• PAT BARKER'S

Regeneration

A READER'S GUIDE

KARIN E. WESTMAN

CONTINUUM | NEW YORK | LONDON

2001

The Continuum International Publishing Group Inc
370 Lexington Avenue, New York, NY 10017

The Continuum Intrernational Publishing Group Ltd
The Tower Building, 11 York Road, London SE1 7NX

www.continuumbooks.com

Printed in the United States of America

Library of Congress Cataloging-in-Publication Data

Westman, Karin E.
  Pat Barker's Regeneration / Karin E. Westman.
    p. cm. — (Continuum contemporaries)
  Includes bibliographical references.
  ISBN 0-8264-5230-2 (alk. paper)
  1. Barker, Pat. Regeneration. 2. Biographical fiction,
English—History and criticism. 3. Sassoon, Siegfried, 1886–1967—In
literature. 4. Rivers, W. H. R. (William Halse Rivers), 1864–1922—In
literature. 5. World War, 1914–1918—Literature and the war.   I.
Title. II. Series.
 PR6052.A6488 R48 2001
 823'.914—dc21

                                                        2001032575

Contents

The Novelist

Most discussions of Pat Barker's novels begin with her biography and with good reason, given the intersections of her life and her art. Barker's fiction draws upon her experiences growing up in the North of England, transmuting elements of her life into the lives of her characters.

Born Patricia Margaret Drake on May 8 1943, Barker spent her early years in her birthplace, Thornaby-on-Tees, near the Northeast industrial town of Middlesbrough.[1] Barker lived her first seven years on a chicken farm with her mother, her mother's mother, and her mother's second husband, a slaughterman. Barker never knew her father or much about him. Her mother, Moira, met Barker's father while she was in the Wrens (the Women's Royal Naval Service), but it seems unlikely they were ever married (Wyatt-Brown, 1996, 57). Barker was told that her father was in the Royal Air Force during World War II and a few other details, but she never had a sense of who he really was. Moira was ready to give Barker up for adoption, but Barker's grandmother "found it inconceivable that any part of your family should be given away," Barker explains to interviewer Donna Perry. Even though the household was "as poor as it's possible to be in England," Barker tells interviewer Amanda Smith, her grandmother was determined to keep Barker a part of it.[2]

Because of the social stigma of bearing an illegitimate child in the 1940s, Moira came to think of her daughter as a sister. "She explained me away as her kid sister or niece so often that she ultimately forgot who I was," Barker tells interviewer Donna Perry. When her mother married and moved away from the farm, Barker willingly remained with her grandparents and helped her grand-mother at a fish-and-chips shop, serving their Teeside customers. The strong, hard-working women who appear in her novels have an antecedent, then, in this working class home that was "entirely run by women" (Smith, 1984). Along with her grandmother, Barker tells Perry, she also "had a whole string of great-aunts who used to get together and quarrel about things that happened when they were growing up in Victorian England." To have grown up beside these women, all "arguing about a past that was very much alive to them," provided Barker with an early view of history as the result of contested stories and multiple voices.

Barker loved to read as a young girl. Thanks to her local library, she was able to supplement the meager offerings of the living room shelves with a wider range of reading materials. The only books at home were her grandfather's set of pre-World War I encyclopedias, whose out-dated information soon taught her to be skeptical of material labeled as "truth"; the shelves held some spiritualist Sunday-school manuals, too, because her grandmother's first hus-band had been a spiritualist medium (Goring, 1998). The local library, then, provided a welcome change, if some restrictions: "I was always furious that the public library wouldn't let me take a book back the same day and get another one out," Barker remarked to interviewer Jane Shilling. To supplement the public library's offerings, Barker also belonged to a ha'penny lending library

(Grove, 1995). During these years, she read "soppy adult romances" but also L. M. Montgomery's *Emily* books, about a young girl who wants to be a writer (Stoffman, 1998). By age eleven Barker had decided, like Emily, to become a writer, and she even wrote her first novel, a romance set in Ruritania, which she later threw away. "It was probably a work of genuis," Barker says with a laugh to interviewer Rosemary Goring, adding, "Of comic genius."

About this time, Barker began attending a strict local girls' grammar school with the help of her grandmother's hard-earned money. Though she enjoyed school, Barker has not spoken directly of her time there. Her comments about her young hero Colin, from *The Man Who Wasn't There*, may shed light on her own experiences, since they both cross class lines to go to a local grammar school: "At the time [in the 1940s], the grammar schools saw themselves as taking kids from poorer cultures and giving them a culture. The idea that they *had* a culture wasn't recognized." Barker's academic success at the grammar school nonetheless won her a scholarship to the London School of Economics and Political Science, where she chose a major in international history, specializing in diplomatic history. Yet as Barker told interviewer Amanda Smith in 1984, she has never really felt comfortable in the university environment: "I was alienated from the academic setting, not at home in it. This is something I still feel. I've never quite belonged in any of the settings in which I superficially seem to belong."

After she graduated from the LSE in 1965, Barker trained as a teacher at Neville's Cross College in Durham and then taught A-level history, politics, and English in further education courses to earn a living. She also returned home in order to care for her dying grandmother (Becker, 1999). While teaching in Middlesborough in 1969, she met David Barker, her future husband and twenty years her senior. A professor of zoology at the University of Durham (now retired), he has always encouraged her literary career — even rescuing, as Sharon Carson notes, "the discarded manuscript of her first novel from the trash" (46). Barker describes his contributions to interviewer Amanda Smith: "he's very pleased, very helpful, very supportive." Furthermore, she adds, "He's an excellent reader, because he doesn't know the critical terms — he just knows whether he wants to go on reading." "[H]e is my first reader at the end," Barker tells interviewer Donna Perry, "And my most important reader." Although she wrote a few thrillers after university, Barker did not believe they were successful (Shilling, 1998). Barker returned to fiction writing in earnest in her early thirties after the birth of her two children: her son John (now 32 years old) and her daughter Anna (now 28 years old). Her resolve came on the heels of her decision to give up full-time teaching in order to care for her daughter (Rodd, 1993). Barker believes the two acts — giving birth and returning to writing — were connected: "It was an immense creative liberation for me to have a baby," if also, she adds, "immense pressure" and "discipline". She was dissatisfied, though, with her current writing, which was "modeled on the 'refined and sensitive' novels of the middle class" (Carson, 1997 46).

PERMISSION TO WRITE

The year 1979 was a turning point: Barker attended her first creative writing course at the Arvon Foundation in the Lumb Bank in Yorkshire. The course was taught by the writer Angela Carter, who, according to Barker, gave her "permission to write" about the people and issues she knew best: working class men and women in the industrial and post-industrial Northeast of England. In retrospect, Barker feels her education hindered her writing rather than helping it, as she explains to Amanda Smith: "In a way, my education was almost a superficial experience. It isn't what I draw on at all in my writing." Trying to write "the sort of thing I'd been educated to admire," Barker tells Smith that it was as though she was "writing very much with the surface veneer that had been put on me by the education I'd undergone, instead of out of the experiences of my life." Angela Carter not only got Barker writing about the life she knew best, but Carter also sent Barker's manuscript for her novel *Union Street* to Carmen Callil at Virago Press. Callil was impressed and willing to publish Barker's work, and Barker soon acquired her first British agent, Curtis Brown.

The publication of *Union Street* (1982) by Virago Press landed Barker a place on Granta's 20 "Best of Young British Novelists," an honor shared by authors such as Salman Rushdie, Martin Amis, and Julian Barnes. The novel also garnered the 1983 Fawcett Prize. As the story of seven women from the Teeside neighborhood of her youth, Barker's first novel offers an unflinching look at the often grim yet unbowed lives of women who range in age from teen to old-age pensioner. Well-received upon publication, it earned Barker's fiction her trademark epithet of "gritty social realism." *Union Street* had the further fortune — or perhaps misfortune — of being made into a film, *Stanley and Iris* (1990), starring Jane Fonda and Robert DeNiro. Originally produced under the title *Letters* and due for release in the United States in the fall of 1989, the film was retitled *Stanley and Iris* and opened in February of 1990. Barker tells Donna Perry in 1988 that she "was very happy with the script," though she wondered how feminists might feel about the changes to the end of the novel's plot. By their second interview in 1991, Barker is more astringent in her comments about a studio's translation of a novel for the screen: "They buy a book for certain qualities and then when they are trying to write the screenplay they get terrified of those qualities — they screen them all out — and produce something totally innocuous and you wonder why." Husband David offers a more succinct summation: "About 2 percent of the movie comes from the book." The book itself, however, established Barker as a voice in contemporary women's writing.

Barker's second novel, *Blow Your House Down* (Virago, 1984), followed on the success of her first. Not optioned for film, *Blow Your House Down* was adapted for the stage. Like *Union Street*, *Blow Your House Down* painted the portrait of a neighborhood of working class women in the North, though their type of work was a more blunt representation of women's social and economic situation. The novel's plot is inspired by Peter Sutcliffe's killing of thirteen and maiming of seven women, mostly prostitutes. The reader follows the narratives of various women, several of whom are prostitutes and all of whom must keep working, regardless of the threat that the "Yorkshire Ripper" presents to their lives. Barker's second novel was written, as Barker tells Amanda Smith, to "see life" through a woman's eyes and to address the intersection of gender, violence, and class. Her goal was "to make the reader get right inside these women and say, look, their lives are real, they are individual, they are valuable," regardless of their social class. When asked by Donna Perry about the role of female friendships in *Blow Your House Down*, Barker's response indicates how the experiences of wartime were already contributing to her thinking about society and social change:

If you look at what women in *Blow Your House Down* are doing for one another, there is support, but it is support for the status quo. When I was writing, I was thinking that they shared the kind of humor men had in the trenches, fighting a war that should not have been fought. Women who are tremendously supportive of a woman being battered, giving support on how to deal with it, are not helping her get out of it. There's a stoicism without any idea of what the alternatives are. These friendships were serving exactly the same purpose as men's friendships in World War I.

Never offering easy answers to tough political questions, Barker's second novel takes risks in its bleak, often ambivalent presentation of women's lives, risks that continue to provoke discussion both in and outside of the classroom.[3]

Barker's third and fourth novels increase the breath and depth of her realistic portraits of British society. *Liza's England* (Virago, 1986), first published as *The Century's Daughter*, follows the life of one woman across the twentieth century. Born on the stroke of midnight in the year 1900, Liza Jarrett's life offers a window onto the experiences of working class women in the Northeast of England. Interspersed with Liza's retelling and remembrances of her past is the story of a contemporary social worker, Stephen, whose friendship with the aged Liza offers him a counterpoint to his struggles with the working class kids he tries to help, his dying father, and his relationship with his partner, who is working abroad. *The Man Who Wasn't There* (Virago, 1989) also selects one character for its focus, closely following the young protagonist, Colin, who rather resembles an early Billy Prior from the upcoming *Regeneration*.[4] Grappling with his place as an illegitimate child in a post–World War II world, Colin imagines himself as the hero (or, perhaps, anti-hero) of spy and war stories reminiscent of the popular movies he sees with his friends. His imagined scenes are represented in the novel's narrative in the form of play or film scripts, and they incorporate details and images from his "real" life at that moment in time. The "Man" of the title is a haunting presence in Colin's waking life and holds multiple meanings for Colin: he is a figure of betrayal, Colin's missing father, and the man Colin might or might not become. Barker's fourth novel is therefore interested in boundaries—boundaries between reality and imagination, between masculinity and femininity, between heroism and self-interest, between youth and maturity, between fiction and drama.

Until the publication of *Regeneration*, then, Barker's work was received under the "regional" label, with the further designations of "women's fiction" and "working-class fiction," offering what *New York Times* reviewer Claudia Roth Pierpoint calls an "anti–Merchant Ivory view of English civilization." Barker tells interviewer Amanda Smith that her choice of material certainly placed her outside existing trends, much to many reviewers' dismay: "I think it's a very foreign world to a lot of London-based publishers and critics — it's regional, it's working class, it's female, for God's sake, and those are not three things that they are particularly in favor of." While regional novels about the working classes were popular in the 1960s, to write such novels in the 1980s, Barker says, means that "you are thought of as doing something that is terribly old-fashioned." Of course, Barker's novels hardly offer the same portrait of working class women found in the pages of John Osborne, John Braine, David Storey, and other popular authors of the post-war period — a feminist difference which complicates Barker's place as a regional, working-class author. *The Man Who Wasn't There* complicated Barker's status as a feminist author for many readers, who in turn criticized her for "deserting the cause" of feminism when she switched to a male protagonist. Barker refutes such a view, saying, "I never thought for a second that feminism is only about women." If her multiple interests in region, class, and gender sometimes stymied the ability of her British reviewers to "place" her, her early work has been consistently well-received in the Unites States, a fact that surprised Barker's editor at Virago, Carmen Callil. Thirty one American publishers were "terrified by the Englishness" of early works like *Union Street*, but Faith Sale at Putnam took the risk and with winning results. "It's very interesting to be a regional author and yet to be better understood abroad," Barker observes to Amanda Smith at the conclusion of their interview.

REGENERATION

Barker had expected her next novel to develop from *The Man Who Wasn't There* and to explore "a man who is plagued by an irrational sense of guilt," since she had been immersing herself in Dostoevsky (Perry, "Going Home," 1991). Instead, Barker wrote *Regeneration* (Viking, 1991). Comments in several interviews suggest that Barker's turn towards men and war was a direct response to critics's comments about her previous novels: "I was fed up with being patronised," she tells Candice Rodd in 1993, "sooner or later some idiot critic says: But uh, can she do men? — as though that were some kind of Everest. I took a very conscious decision to change what I wrote about." Barker says that she has always felt she "could do either"; she does not subscribe to the view of some women novelists like Fay Weldon who "says men are a different species" (Perry, *Backtalk* 1993 51). Barker therefore acknowledges that *Regeneration* is a change from her previous work, but she also emphasizes its connections to her earlier novels: "I did seem to be setting off at right angles, which wasn't actually true. The themes in 'Regeneration' are also the themes of books like 'Union Street' — they're about trauma, whether it's experienced by working-class people or aristocrats" (Becker, 1999), "about trauma and recovery."Barker sees *Regeneration* as consistent with a larger feminist project — "I think that analysis of men's dependency and their lack of autonomy in that war, a study of why they suffered from hysterical symptoms rather than paranoia is a feminist analysis" — even if she does not return to the same neighborhood and people as her earlier novels (Perry, *Backtalk* 1993 52).

In selecting 1917 as the time frame for *Regeneration*, Barker returned to one of the periods she describes in *Liza's England*, developing that one moment of time for the whole of the novel and crafting its narrative from multiple points of view rather than Liza's single one. The decision to write historical fiction posed a challenge, Barker explains to interviewer Wera Reusch: "The historical novel really forces you to ask yourself all the time what is there in human nature that doesn't otherwise change, because that is what you have to write about because otherwise nobody is interested in reading what you have written anyway." Such writing also raises questions about verisimilitude, especially for a realist writer. While writing the dialogue for the *Regeneration* trilogy, Barker says that she "avoided the kind of language they spoke because at least on our side of the trenches there was this sort of farcical humour which would not be appreciated today," "a black humour," "a kind of black laughter, laughter on the other side of the despair" (Reusch, 2000). Though Barker uses the label "historical novel" when speaking with Reusch, she has also challenged that label in other interviews because it suggests that the novel's events are past, no longer a part of the present: "I don't accept that *The Eye in the Door* and *Regeneration* are historical novels," Barker tells interviewer Candice Rodd, "They're about a period of the world's history that we have never come to terms with." Though Barker's rejection of the label "historical novel" seems to contradict her statement to Reusch, it also help us understand another of Barker's statements in the same interview, when she explains her choice of historical period for *Regeneration*: "I chose the First World War because it's come to stand in for other wars [. . . .] [I]t's come to stand for the pain of all wars." For Barker, then, the First World War allows for both the realism of a particular moment in history and the symbolism of a culture's experience of war. The designation "historical novel" for *Regeneration* is appropriate, so long as we see its past history as part of our present.

Barker's interest in the First World War is longstanding, as she tells Donna Perry in *Backtalk*, even if the idea for *Regeneration* arrived through "several channels." Barker first read the poetry of

Wilfred Owen and Siegfried Sassoon in her teens and Dr. W. H. R. Rivers's *Conflict and Dream* in her early twenties, but that interest laid dormant for many years: "I had always wanted to write about Rivers and shell shock and about the first world war, too. That first thing I ever wrote was a terribly bad poem about the first world war when I was eleven. So the urge to write was there, but I wanted to wait until I could find a sufficiently original way of doing it". Her husband, David, was involved in this book project much earlier than other ones. First, he introduced Barker to another side of Rivers than the psychologist represented in her early reading of *Conflict and Dream*: he introduced her to the Rivers he knew from his own research, Rivers the scientist, who conducted neurological experiments with Henry Head. As Barker's own research progressed, Rivers the anthropologist soon added a third layer to his character and her ideas for the book (Quinn, 1995). David was also involved earlier in her preparations for writing because, as Barker explains, "the actual story of Rivers was historical, and he knew the story." David would accompany her for her field research, and together they explored the battlefields and library archives of the war years: "I'd grab the car," David tells interview Donna Perry in *Backtalk*, "and find a place on a map and all that sort of thing".

Barker was particularly drawn to Rivers's work because he was a "complex and compassionate man, ahead of his time": "He was the first to recognize the links between men breaking down in battle and the hysteria, as it was then described, which was experienced by women in peacetime" (Davidson, 1997). In her interview with Wera Reusch, Barker briefly recounts what captured her interest in Rivers's history:

he was a psychiatrist who joined the army in 1915, as soon as he could. He was an anthropologist before the war, but he had a medical degree, so he went back to practising medicine for the duration of the war. And he was a very humane, a very compassionate person who was tormented really by the suffering he saw, and very sceptical about the war, but at the same time he didn't feel he could go the whole way and say no, stop.

Such varied if complementary interests, combined with his study of cultures through the lens of gender, fascinated Barker. Though Rivers has been disregarded for many years by his profession, he has since re-emerged as an important contributor to early twentieth-century social anthropology (Wyatt-Brown, 1996, 58). One of the sources Barker cites in her "Author's Note," Elaine Showalter's *The Female Malady* (1985), was one of the studies that brought Rivers back into critical prominence for his theories on the link between gender and war neurosis.

Family history was yet another "channel" that flowed toward Barker's creation of *Regeneration*. Barker has clear childhood memories of times she would "stick her finger" into the wound her grandfather received while an officer's servant during the First World War. His "horrific scar" was the result of being bayoneted but then living to tell the tale. Her grandfather's officer "shot the German between the eyebrows, which meant that he didn't have the chance to twist the bayonet and pull it out, which is the bit that really does all the damage." Barker's grandfather "survived, but he had to lie on the battlefield and he got flies all around and maggots in the wound," and then he "lay on the floor of the hospital for hours and hours before he was treated." Though she often saw the physical scar, Barker only heard the stories of her grandfather's war experiences near the end of his life, because, as Barker explains to Donna Perry, "they were so horrific that he didn't want to tell them before then" (*Backtalk* 1993 47). These stories—and her grandfather's reticence—provide the physical and emotional underpinning of the characters' experiences in *Regeneration*, as well as Barker's next three books.

With the publication of *The Eye in the Door* (1993) and *The Ghost Road* (1995), Barker completed what is now called the *Regeneration* trilogy. Both novels won critical recognition as well as the praise of general readers. *The Eye in the Door* won the 1993 Guardian Fiction Prize, and *The Ghost Road* won the prestigious and highly publicized Booker Prize for Fiction in 1995. As sequels to *Regeneration*, the novels follow the characters of the first novel into the last year of the war; the focus of *The Eye in the Door* falls more towards the character of Billy Prior and the difficulties faced by conscientious objectors, while *The Ghost Road* provides an extended look at Rivers's past as an anthropologist in Melanesia as well as following Sassoon, Owen, and Prior in the war's present. In the wake of Barker's success, all three books were published in one volume in 1996 under the title *The Regeneration Trilogy*. *Another World* (1998), Barker's eighth novel, evolved from her contact with war veterans after the *Regeneration* trilogy, particularly when filming a documentary for the BBC (Becker, 1999). Her grandfather's last years also contributed to the depiction of Geordie, a World War I veteran, who believes the pain of his cancer is the legacy of his physical and emotional wounds from the war. Set partially in the present of Geordie's relatives yet linked to the past of World War I through Geordie's vivid memories, *Another World*, in Barker's words, shows her "trying to knit the two strands together," of past and present (Becker, 1999).

THE WRITING PROCESS

Regardless of which novel Barker is working towards, the decision to write begins with the characters' voices. There is "a long period before the start of writing, of bringing the characters to life and knowing them," Barker tells Perry in "Going Home": "When they start talking to each other, you start writing." The process of drafting marks the next important step: "By the end of the first draft, it's full of wrong turnings," and "by then I've seen the book I ought to have written instead of the book I have written" (Becker, 1999). As of 1988, Barker would "try to from 8:30 to 12:45 every day," and she had switched from "an old, smug little typewriter" to a computer ("Going Home"). Given her own experiences as a writer, Barker firmly believes that writing grows out of one's life: "I think the starting point is inevitably always something in your own life," she tells Donna Perry, "just as the source of every single character you create has to be yourself. But quite often you are going off on a tangent— taking a fact in your own life and saying, 'What if . . . ' and from that point you are going away from your own life at right angles, although the bedrock of the book was your own experience" (*Backtalk* 1993 46). Though Barker explains that she is "not interested in writing autobiography in any way, shape, or form," she does feel that "at the end of the day when you look at the books on the shelf they are—for every writer, not just for me—the spiritual autobiography."

Barker tells interviewer Amanda Smith that there are "very few" authors who influence her, since "there are very few who are trying to write about the kind of things in England that I want to write about." Asked by Robert McCrum about the writers she admires, however, Barker responds, "Contemporary writers, mainly poetry: Hughes, Heaney, Simon Armitage, Glyn Maxwell." For Barker, poetry provides an "intensity of language," a way to "remind yourself of how precisely language can be used." To E. Jane Dickson, Barker has spoken of her regard for the poetry of Ted Hughes, whose work provided a "shock of recognition" when she read his first collection, *The Hawk in the Rain* (1957), in her teens, and she identified with the realism of his descriptions. Barker has formed a close friendship with author Wendy Robertson, whose characters inhabit the same world as Barker's. Of their friendship, Barker says, "Being working-class northern girls we can take a lot about each other for granted. We have a shared passion for people who have been forced to the margins of history and have essentially been silenced." More generally, Barker emphasizes the importance of her connections with other writers: "Friendships between writers are essential because writing is an incredibly isolating thing to do. You can take so much for granted when you meet another writer, like those 3 o'clock morning doubts. It helps to spend so much time with someone who knows exactly what it's like" (O'Connell, 2001). American women authors, particularly African-American authors, have also provided some company along her path, either in person or through their writings. Barker often names Alice Walker, Toni Morrison, and Gloria Naylor in her interviews.

Though she does not name her mentor as an influence, Angela Carter's presence certainly lurks behind some of Barker's more humorous scenes, with their gallows humor, earthy physicality, and vaudeville moments. T. S. Eliot's poetry lingers in moments of *Regeneration*'s narrative: there are echoes of *The Waste Land* in Madge's desire to get false teeth (110) and in a description of days that are slapped down "like a fortune-teller with a deadly pack of cards" (185), as well as echoes of "Preludes" and "The Love Song of J. Alfred Prufrock" in the "insidious" streets that smell of steaks (86). In a house whose walls are lined with books in alphabetical order—"Manning, Mantel, Murdoch," "Wilson, Wodehouse, Woolf" (Grove, 1995)—it comes as no surprise that Barker firmly believes in reading men as well as women authors. To only read about women would be to suggest, in Barker's words, that "feminist writing and feminism are exclusively about women," an idea that runs counter to her views on gender and social change (Perry, "Going Home").

LIFE AFTER THE BOOKER

The *Regeneration* trilogy, thanks to its many awards and prizes (especially the Booker Prize), has brought Barker a fair amount of media attention and fame that, unfortunately, often take her away from her writing. Barker's Booker win came in a year of calm between otherwise stormy Booker seas, as *New York Times* reviewer Eva Hoffman reported. Eschewing the usual scandals and polemics, the judges awarded Barker the prize for *The Ghost Road* over the other favorite, Salman Rushdie's *The Moor's Last Sigh*, as well as Justin Cartwright's *In Every Face I Meet*, Barry Unsworth's *Morality Play*, and Tim Winton's *The Riders* — a list that was "militantly uncontroversial," according to the *Independent*. The ensuing year hardly felt calm to Barker, who describes the Booker win as a "tornado" (Shilling, 1998).[5] Increasingly part of the literary establishment, by 1995 Barker had switched agents to become part of the "Aitken & Stone (and Andrew Wylie) literary stable," alongside such well-known contemporaries as Salman Rushdie, Fay Weldon, and Martin Amis (Grove, 1995).

The press has consequently pounced with characteristic energy upon Barker and her work, often rather surprised at what they have found. Barker is frequently described in interviews as "motherly," looking like "somebody's Mum, come down to London for a shopping expedition to Selfridges and a look round the Sargent exhibit," or as someone "projecting an image of such utter normality," "a picture of middle-aged respectability." Appearances, though, can be deceiving. Interviewer and book critic Rosemary Goring speaks of Barker's "no-nonsense forthrightness," a bluntness belied by the bourgeois domesticity of her home in Durham, and also of her laughter, which bubbles forth in most interviews. Barker has been quite tolerant of the press and the attention a Booker win brings: "I would probably knock the Booker on the head if I could think of an equally successful way of promoting literary fiction," she tells Helena de Bertodano of the *Sunday Telegraph*, "But I can't." In an interview with Valerie Grove, Barker describes book prizes as a "necessary evil." Interviews seem to fall into that category as well. Goring remarks that "as [Barker] gives an interview there is the air of a duty being performed. Though she is very welcoming, and talks expansively, warmly, there is a degree of restraint, a sense of life suspended and, you suspect, time wasted." Barker's preference, then, for "things to be very quiet" and her desire to keep to the peace of her home in Durham often wait in line behind the obligations of success.

In the early 1990s, Barker returned to become one of the teachers for the writing workshop where she discovered her own voice. The work was "very, very hard, because it's all about establishing the writer's voice," but a kind of teaching that she enjoys. "You have to be very, very delicate, though," she adds to Donna Perry: "It's like being Rivers because you are dealing with terribly explosive materials" (*Backtalk*, 1993 60–1). Awards and recognition continue to arrive at her door. In 1998, Barker received the honorary degree of Doctor of Letters from the University of Durham. (Though Barker was first announced as an honorary graduate in 1997, the date of the ceremony was rescheduled to the following June.) She also participated that year in the Cheltenham Literary Festival alongside 300 other authors, including Sebastian Faulks, John Fowles, Julian Barnes, and William Boyd. Given the popularity of the *Regeneration* trilogy and the UK's renewed interest in the First World War, Barker often finds herself in demand for its topic. On 11 November 2000, for instance, she presented the Armistice Day programmes for BBC Knowledge. Her most recent novel, *Border Crossing* (2001), is a "brilliant, lean piece of story-telling," according to Suzi Feay of the *Independent*—a psychological thriller that is already receiving many favorable reviews and marks her continued interest in psychology, past acts, and accountability.

While Barker's two recent novels mostly take place in the present day, Barker tells interviewer Wera Reusch that she does anticipate writing historical novels again: "I think there is a lot to be said for writing about history, because you can sometimes deal with contemporary dilemmas in a way people are more open to because it is presented in this unfamiliar guise, they don't automatically know what they think about it, whereas if you are writing about a contemporary issue on the nose, sometimes all you do is activate people's prejudices." At age 58, happily situated in Durham in a house filled with books, Barker looks ahead with pleasure to disguising contemporary dilemmas within her prose.

2

The Novel

Regeneration takes place at Craiglockhart War Hospital in Edinburgh, Scotland in 1917, between the months of July and November. As Barker indicates in her "Author's Note" at the end of the novel, several characters were real people who are well-known in the fields of science and literature: Dr W. H. R. Rivers, Dr Lewis Yelland, Dr Henry Head, Siegfried Sassoon, Wilfred Owen, and Robert Graves. In her blending of fact and fiction, Barker focuses on the relationships between her characters, as they negotiate their roles in a culture not only at war with Germany, but also with itself. The novel's themes therefore range across many areas of society, highlighting cultural tensions brought to the surface by the war: questions about duty, authority, psychology, gender, homosexuality, class, love, memory, the value of individual life, and the value of the imagination. This range of themes in turn marks the novel's unusual place in the canon of literature about World War I, as well as its contribution to contemporary historical fiction.

CONFLICTING DUTIES

While many reviewers identify Siegfried Sassoon as the main character of *Regeneration*, Barker herself names Dr. W. H. R. Rivers.[6] Both characters, however, share a similar burden: conflicting duties. The idea of "duty" was a mainstay of cultural values during the nineteenth century; if on the wane by the turn of the century, it returned in full force with the onset of war in 1914, as recruiting posters urged all British citizens to fulfill their obligations to King and country. But what if duty for one's country came into conflict with other British ideals, like the duty to individual freedom and the duty to fight for one's beliefs? Sassoon's letter to his commanding officer, titled "Finished with the War, A *Soldier's Declaration*," asks these difficult questions. Reproduced on the first page of the novel, the letter introduces the reader right away to the theme of conflicting duties. We join Rivers in reading Sassoon's argument against war, as Sassoon questions his duty to his country, if that duty must come at the expense of his duty to fellow citizens who are dying and suffering in vast numbers each day. By the end of the novel, Rivers helps Sassoon resolve the tension between these two duties by encouraging Sassoon to return to war for the sake of the men under his command. Along the way, however, Rivers must acknowledge his increasing sympathy for Sassoon's political beliefs and the conflicting duties which arise from his paradoxical role as a "military doctor."

The conflict Rivers experiences as a doctor for the Royal Army Medical Corps opens the novel's narrative, as he reads Sassoon's "Declaration" at Colonel Bryce's request. Already sensing that Sassoon "doesn't *sound* as if he's gibbering" (4), Rivers finds himself thinking, "Misguided the Declaration might well be, but it was not deluded, illogical or incoherent" (8). All too aware that "[h]e *wanted* Sassoon to be ill" (8), Rivers soon realizes that to acknowledge the sanity of Sassoon's position means he must further question the sanity of his own support of the war. Taking Sassoon's case therefore not only places Rivers in the middle of a raging debate between Medical Officers "about the freedom of the individual conscience in wartime, and the role of the army physician in 'treating' the man who refused to fight" (8–9). Taking Sassoon's case also requires Rivers to decide for himself how he feels about the war — whether it is the duty of the nation to fight, even when there's no end or gain in sight. For the next several months, Rivers becomes his own case study, assessing the stress these conflicting duties play upon his life at Craiglockhart, as he struggles to assist Sassoon and many others to come to terms with their emotional responses to the war.

Rivers's integrity of character precludes him from lying to or manipulating Sassoon once he confirms that Sassoon suffers from none of the usual nervous disorders displayed by other patients at Craiglockhart, but his integrity also complicates his ability to perform his duty as a Medical Officer. This conflict of duties appears in their first interview, when Rivers fully admits to Sassoon's sanity: "of course you're not mad" (14), he assures Sassoon, adding, "You seem to have a very powerful *anti*-war neurosis" (15). Their shared laughter at Rivers's joke, however, is quickly dispelled by Rivers's assertion of his role as army doctor: "You realize, don't you, that it's my duty to . . . to try to change that? I can't pretend to be neutral" (15). Further meetings with Sassoon show Rivers that his difficulty will not reside in being "neutral" but in fulfilling his duty as a Medical Officer. When questioned by his fellow Medical Officers about Sassoon's case, Rivers emphatically states his goals: "He's a mentally and physically healthy man. It's *his* duty to go back, and it's *my* duty to see he does" (73). In the privacy of his own thoughts, Rivers comes to different conclusions:

As soon as you accepted that the man's breakdown was a consequence of his war experience rather than of his own innate weakness, then inevitably war became the issue. And the therapy was a test, not only of the genuineness of the individual's symptoms, but also of the validity of the demands the war was making on him. Rivers had survived partly by suppressing his awareness of this. But then along came Sassoon and made the justifiability of the war a matter for constant, open debate, and that suppression was not longer possible. (115–16)

Rivers is acutely sympathetic to Sassoon's view of the war, in part because he feels constant tension between his obligation to make his patients remember horrifying parts of their pasts and his desire to prevent further suffering. This tension, suppressed when possible, surfaces in one of Rivers's dreams, linking his pre-war experiments with his friend Dr. Henry Head on nerve regeneration to his current experimental treatments on war neurosis. Significantly, Rivers conceptualizes the tension as a question of "duty" (47): the duty of the doctor to create pain, in contrast to the duty of a fellow human being to prevent pain. Rivers, then, is caught between two sets of conflicting duties as he seeks to help his patients: the duties of doctor and officer, and the duties of a fellow human sufferer and a doctor. Sassoon's presence at Craiglockhart brings both sets of duties into focus.

Keeping such conflicting thoughts to himself, Rivers persuades Sassoon to accept the war by allowing Sassoon to dwell on the men he has left in the fields of France and by playing off of Sassoon's "absolutely corrosive hatred of civilians" (16). Providing Sassoon with more clean sheets, golf, and good club food than Sassoon can stand, Rivers prophesies for Sassoon the results of prolonged resistance: "If you maintain your protest, you can expect to spend the remainder of the war in a state of Complete. Personal. Safety. [. . .] You don't think you might find being safe while other people *die* rather difficult?" (36). Sassoon does find it difficult. To get back to France, perhaps to risk his life only so he can die, Sassoon willingly acknowledges to the medical board that he feels it his "duty" to go back (246), regardless of how he might feel about the war. Rivers is left wondering if he has done his duty as a doctor by letting Sassoon go.

CHOOSING SIDES

The evening before Sassoon's medical board, Sassoon and Rivers have a telling exchange:

Rivers took the only available chair, and stretched out his legs towards the empty grate.

"Well, how do you feel about tomorrow?"

"All right. Still nothing from the War Office?"

"No, I'm afraid not. You'll just have to trust us."

"Us? You're sure you don't mean 'them'?"

"You know I'll go on doing anything I can for you." (203)

Though Sassoon has trusted Rivers since their first interview, even he questions whether Rivers is one of "us" or one of "them" within the world of Craiglockhart War Hospital. The mute Billy Prior, a recent arrival, is certain that Rivers must be one of "them," and Prior's behavior tests Rivers's identity as "doctor" in ways that Sassoon and his "Declaration" do not. Seeing their relationship as a battle which someone must "win," Prior presumes the game is already fixed for Rivers's success. Rivers tries to correct him: "This may come as a shock, Mr Prior, but I had been rather assuming we were on the same side." Prior responds with a smile: "This may come as a shock, Dr Rivers, but I had been *rather assuming* that we were not" (80). Parroting Rivers's words and theories back to him, Prior repeatedly forces Rivers to assume the role of patient, much to Rivers's dismay.

Prior struggles to control the doctor/patient relationship from his first silent encounter with Rivers, using only a pencil, a pad of paper, and a series of shrugs. Frustrated by Prior's combative manner, Rivers finds himself wielding power in atypical ways, correcting Prior's spelling ("Two l's in 'physically,' Mr Prior") and drawing a spoon across the back of Prior's throat to check for sensitivity (42). During their first spoken conversation, Prior challenges the dynamics of the professional relationship by asking Rivers the same question Rivers just posed to him. He soon voices his frustration directly: "I don't see why it has to *be* like this anyway. [. . .] All the questions from *you*, all the answers from *me*. Why can't it be both ways?" (50). After Rivers explains that most patients in despair do not usually care about their doctors' feelings, Prior retorts, "Well, all I can say is I'd rather talk to a real person than a a strip of empathic wallpaper" (51). Rivers smiles at Prior's barb, but finds himself taking a *"[d]eep breath"* as he continues the interview (51). Unable to put Prior at ease, as he does Sassoon and other patients, Rivers's good-natured bedside manner is sorely taxed, and he encounters qualities in himself for which he must apologize later.

Prior's relentless interest in Rivers — "how quickly Prior pounced on any item of personal information," Rivers reflects during one conversation (64) — threatens the security of Rivers's professional assurance. Being aware of this dynamic does nothing to lessen Rivers's discomfort. When Rivers finds Prior reading *The Todas*, the anthropological study Rivers wrote before the war, Rivers must strive to keep calm:

He told himself there was no reason why Prior shouldn't read one of his books, or all of them for that matter. There was no rational reason for him to feel uneasy. He handed the book back. "Wouldn't you prefer something lighter? You are ill, after all."

Prior leaned back against his pillows, his eyes gleaming with amusement. "Do you know, I *knew* you were going to say that. Now how did I know that?" (65)

Prior's control of himself and of the conversation is rarely thwarted. We even learn that "[i]t was a point of honor with him to lie to Rivers at least once during every meeting" (87). Any respect he feels for Rivers is expressed backward or indirectly, as when he remarks to Rivers, "I find myself wanting to impress you. Pathetic, isn't it?" (64). Prior's sarcastic, caustic tone only breaks when he is forced to admit to needing assistance, either physical (his asthma) or emotional (his embarrassment at Rivers's proffered apology, his relief and frustration upon learning the event that precipitated his mutism). Otherwise, Prior makes Rivers all too aware that there is a thin line between being a doctor and being a patient.

"WHAT DO YOU DO WHEN THE DOCTOR BREAKS DOWN?"

Anderson, an Army surgeon and one of Rivers's patients, poses this question to Rivers, but the question becomes rhetorical when the scene ends without Rivers's reply (31). His question lingers in Rivers's and the reader's minds, though, in light of Rivers's past and present behavior. Rivers's repressed stammer illustrates how the lines of authority are more fluid than fixed and how they are likely to blur at the least opportune time. Like his patients, Rivers must grapple with the legacy of his past, one that represents the control his father held over him and Rivers's efforts to break free from that control.

Whereas Sassoon registers but does not remark upon Rivers's stutter (69), Prior, of course, notices and draws Rivers's attention to it. The opportunity to do so occurs when Rivers explains the class-based differences between those who are mute and those who stammer: private soldiers are more like to be mute, because they do not voice what they desire to say for fear of punishment; officers are more likely to stammer, because they worry what they want to say will be unacceptable. Prior, as a working-class officer, confounds such distinctions, and he presses Rivers to reveal himself as another who confounds such simplistic binaries:

"We-ell, it's interesting that you were mute and that you're one of the very few people in the hospital who *doesn't* stammer."
   "It's even more interesting that you do."
   Rivers was taken aback. "That's d-different."
   "How is it different? Other than that you're on that side of the desk?" (97)

Rivers explains that he has a life-long stammer, which may be genetic, but Prior is not swayed from his purpose. He pushes Rivers to acknowledge the false security of his position: "Now that is lucky, isn't it? Lucky for you, I mean. Because if your stammer was the same as theirs—you might actually have to sit down and work out what it is you've spent fifty years trying not to say" (97). Rivers tries to make light of Prior's accusation—"Is that the end of my appointment for the day, Mr Prior?" (97)—but Prior's statements have their intended effect. For the rest of the day, Rivers finds himself aware of his speech patterns, striving to contain any hint of a stutter.

Rivers's breakdown is hardly unexpected by Rivers or the reader when it finally arrives in chapter 13. Prior's unveiling of Rivers's likely status as "patient" only corroborates Rivers's own close watch on his physical and emotional health in the preceding chapters. All

too aware of his susceptibility, Rivers recognizes the "familiar symptoms" (139) when they wake him in the night, and he knows that
he must inform Bryce. When Bryce arrives, as "brisk and sympathetic" as Rivers himself would be under reversed circumstances,
we get a glimpse of what Rivers will be like as a patient: difficult.
Bryce's command that Rivers take three weeks leave is met by a
"mutinous silence" (140) worthy of Billy Prior. When observing
Prior during one of their sessions, Rivers concludes that "he would
have tackled [the traumas of warfare] in exactly the same way as
Prior" (79). It appears Rivers tackles authority in the same way as
Prior, too.

LIKE FATHER, LIKE SON?

Rivers is more like Prior than he might care to admit, especially as
Rivers contemplates his relationship with patriarchal authorities. At
times, Rivers finds himself oddly sympathetic to Prior's "sharp-
boned alley cat" persona, just as he feels sympathy for his brother's
cat, MacTavish, "a black, battered tom" who is "notably morose"
(151). At other times, Prior's frustration irritates him, perhaps because it reminds Rivers of his own troubled relationship with authority in the guise of his father. Prior's and Rivers's shared anger at
authority, then, not only blurs the socially imposed line between
doctor and patient, but also the line between father and son. Watch-
ing Rivers and Prior, we are asked to see the continuity between
generations, not just the gap.

About thirty years older than his youngest patient, Rivers represents the authority of the father for most men in his care (34), but
Prior does not permit Rivers to play this role with any degree of
ease — hardly surprising, given our knowledge of Prior's past. In Part
I, we witness with Rivers the complex relationships of Prior's family:

a working class father who wants to toughen up his son and hold him to his class's origins, a mother who wants to protect her son and educate him beyond the limits of his class, and their son who loves and hates them both for their efforts. In Part III, when we follow Rivers back to his home parish for part of his leave, we learn the depth of Rivers's anger at his own father, a son's anger which links him to Prior, another angry son. As a speech therapist and a priest (153), Rivers's father embodies the combined patriarchal authorities of family, education, and church. When a young boy, Rivers seethed and finally rebelled against his father's authority when he stuttered his way through a speech in support of Darwin's theories of evolution, forcing his father to listen to the content of his words and not just the way he spoke them. Revisiting such memories of angry rebellion allows Rivers to realize that he has become a "father," an authority of medicine and the military, and that he is now as open to criticism as his own father was to him. This realization changes his view of his father, now dead, but it also forces Rivers to view himself as a fallible figure of authority. He discovers he must always evaluate experience through the eyes of a son and a father.

In aligning his father with three types of patriarchal authority — family, education, church — Rivers further identifies his father as one of many "fathers" of an older generation who are responsible for the present horrors of the war. While studying the familiar Biblical scenes depicted on the stain-glass windows of his family church, Rivers reflects on the "two bloody bargains on which a civilization claims to be based," the crucifixion of Christ and Abraham's sacrifice of his son. The two become representative of one type of bargain, Rivers decides, "*[t]he* bargain," "the one on which all patriarchal societies are founded": "If you, who are young and strong, will obey me, who am old and weak, even to the extent of being prepared to sacrifice your life, then in the course of time you will peacefully inherit, and be able to exact the same obedience from your sons" (149). The failure of this bargain angers Rivers. The current fathers of society have failed to uphold the terms of this social contract, as so many young men die before they can inherit peace and power. More importantly, the war has revealed the contract as inherently false when enacted on so large a scale. As one of society's "fathers," Rivers knows he must use first person plural when he acknowledges to himself that "we're breaking the bargain" (149). He must acknowledge his complicity in the war, even as his identification with his past anger provides him insight through a son's eyes. A patient and a son, he is also a doctor and a father.

AN ETHNOGRAPHY OF GENDER ROLES

The roles of father/son and of doctor/patient are inextricably inter-twined for Rivers because of the type of experimental medicine he has decided to practice. Favoring talking to electric shocks and remembering to forgetting, Rivers engages in conversation with each patient for several weeks. In those conversations, Rivers incor-porates the ethnographic skills he used during his days as an anthro-pologist as he studies the effects of British culture on his patients.[7] The results, as in most ethnographic experiments, have implications for himself as well as the men he studies.

Unlike many of his colleagues who do not believe in shell-shock and consider "nervous" behavior to be a sign of cowardice, Rivers believes the patients he sees at Craiglockhart do indeed suffer from neurosis, a neurosis precipitated by the conditions of warfare but caused by socialized gender roles. The source of men's war neurosis, according to Rivers, is therefore society's compulsory masculinity coming into conflict with the logistics of trench warfare:

Mobilization. The Great Adventure—the real life equivalent of all the
adventure stories they'd devoured as boys—consisted of crouching in a
dugout, waiting to be killed. The war that had promised so much in the
way of "manly" activity had actually delivered "feminine" passivity, and on
a scale that their mothers and sisters had scarcely known. No wonder they
broke down. (107–8)

For Rivers, the parallels between the soldiers' hysteria during war
and women's hysteria during peace are all too clear: in both cases,
"their relatively more confined lives gave them fewer opportunities
of reacting to stress in active and constructive ways" (222). Rivers
also realizes that to make such a claim implicates his own cultural
identity: "In leading his patients to understand that breakdown was
nothing to be ashamed of, [. . .] he was setting himself against the
whole tenor of their upbringing. [. . .] In advising his young patients to abandon the attempt at repression and to let themselves
feel the pity and terror their war experience inevitably evoked, he
was excavating the ground he stood on" (48). Relying on masculine
authority to advise them, Rivers's advice also undermines the authority from which he speaks. He cannot but be affected by treating
his patients, in both personal and cultural terms, if he accepts the
results of his cultural study.

If soldiers are made feminine by their experiences in the
trenches, officers often become maternal figures who provide "domestic" comfort and emotional support as much as stern patriarchs
who meet out justice. Again, Rivers's ethnographic perspective finds
a peace time analogue for the officers' lives, men who spend so
much time "[w]orrying about socks, boots, blisters, food, hot drinks"
that they acquire a "perpetually harried expression": "Rivers had
only ever seen that look in one other place: in the public wards of
hospitals, on the faces of women bringing up large families on very
low incomes [. . .] It was the look of people who are totally respon-

sible for lives they have no power to save" (107). Rivers's cultural insight—his linking of privileged young men to lower class mothers—challenges an essentialist view of gender. The officers' experiences indicate that motherhood is not only a biological role, and Rivers's own experiences confirm this analysis. Treated as much as a mother as a father by Prior and an earlier patient, Layard, Rivers must accept the maternal role some patients assign him during the process of treatment—one he is willing to accept, if reluctantly, in order to help his patients. His willingness to listen to and to provide unconditional comfort for his patients are noted "feminine" and maternal qualities, yet these very qualities make him a successful figure of medical authority for his patients. The best method of treatment requires, then, a redefinition of masculinity, since "[f]ear and tenderness [. . .] were so despised that they could be admitted into consciousness only at the cost of redefining what it meant to be a man" (48). If Rivers is to help his patients escape the shame of their "feminine" behavior and do so effectively, the social expectations for "masculine" behavior must change.

Far from solidifying gendered behavior, then, Barker suggests that the extraordinary culture of war up-ends convention, even requires the exchange of some feminine qualities for the expected masculine ones. Yet this carnivalesque exchange[8] of social roles can only take place *during* war, perhaps even only on the front lines or at Craiglockhart, as Rivers learns when he visits the established Dr Yelland in London. Yelland's presence in *Regeneration* serves as an important reminder to the reader that Rivers's methods and views are indeed experimental and anomalous.[9] Using electric shocks to will patients to speak, walk, and conduct themselves "appropriately," Yelland believes that the men who break down in war would have broken down in any other circumstances (115). For Yelland, the war is therefore not the primary catalyst for his patients' neurosis, as it is in Rivers's view, and socialized gender roles are the answer to the problem, not its source. Eschewing the empathy essential to Rivers's method, Yelland is hardly a strip of "empathic wallpaper." His complete lack of concern for a patient's personal history and emotional state of mind grants him a tunnel vision which horrifies Rivers, even as it forces Rivers to acknowledge some similarities in their goals. Indeed, Yelland's command to his patient, Callan, makes him sound much like Rivers's father sounds to Rivers as a boy: *"You must speak, but I shall not listen to anything you have to say"* (231). Having rejected his father's methods, it seems only consistent for Rivers to reject Yelland's. At the same time, Rivers cannot help noticing similarities between his work and Yelland's, just as he noticed similarities between himself and his father. The methods he and Yelland use might be different, but they "were both *locked in,* every bit as much as their patients were," to the will of the war (238).

In truth, what does make Rivers quite different from Yelland is Rivers's enormous capacity to analyze his own culture and his role in that culture. This capacity grows from his trips to the Solomon Islands as an anthropologist, when some natives whom Rivers was interviewing pose his questions back to him, much as Prior does during his meetings with Rivers. For Rivers, the moment with the islanders showed him "the *Great White God* de-throned," as he tells Henry Head; he realized that British culture was not "the measure of all things, but that *there was no measure*" (242). Rivers's strength as a character comes from his willingness to continue to evaluate himself and others, as well as his willingness to acknowledge how he has been changed by his contact with his patients. As he reviews Sassoon's case file on the eve of his departure, Rivers realizes that "[h]ere in this building, where he had no time to be introverted or self-conscious, where he hardly had a moment to himself at all, the changes had taken place without his knowing. That was not Sieg-fried. That was all of them. Burns and Prior and Pugh and a hundred others" (249). A true ethnographer, Rivers sees himself as a participant in, not an impartial observer of, his work.

"IS IT THE RIGHT *KIND* OF LOVE?"

Rivers's unconventional theories about gender and his knowledge of other cultures' sexual practices make him sympathetic to homosexuality in Britain. Unlike colleagues who might use "a man's private life to discredit his views" on pacifism (55) or to imprison him as a danger to society (204), Rivers finds such methods "despicable" (55). That said, Rivers is quite conventional in his preference to keep silent on the subject. True to the dominant cultural beliefs of the day, the characters in *Regeneration* avoid discussing homosexuality by name. Instead, "the love that dare not speak its name" makes a number of covert appearances through indirect allusions, associations, and jokes, illustrating its role as an absent presence on the cultural landscape. In *The Eye in the Door* and *The Ghost Road*, when the narrative spends more time with the soldiers and citizens of Britain, the physical act of homosexuality makes a much more dramatic appearance. In *Regeneration*, its allusive presence serves as a reminder that outside the walls of Craiglockhart, any deviance from the preferred norms of gendered behavior will not be tolerated.

Rivers is wary of introducing the topic of homosexuality in his conversations with patients, for fear of discomforting them or forcing them to reveal information better left unsaid. Not only was homosexuality illegal in Britain from 1885 until 1967, but the cultural climate of war precluded tolerating sexual acts which might be privately acceptable during peace-time. The frank discussion Rivers and Sassoon have late in the novel about homosexuality explains for the reader why any tolerance that existed before the war has disappeared. While Sassoon expresses the hope that "things were getting better" for homosexuals, Rivers disagrees, noting how the war has reversed any progress: "in war, you've got this enormous emphasis on love between men — comradeship — and everybody approves. But at the same time there's always this little niggle of anxiety. Is it the right *kind* of love? Well, one of the ways you make sure it's the right kind is to make it crystal clear what the penalties for the other kind are" (204). The soldiers' need for "comradeship" (what we now also call homosocial behavior or male bonding) was crucial to survival in war and therefore could not be denied. However, the expression of those male bonds raised some complicated questions about the line between homosocial and homosexual love. To create a clear distinction, any tendencies towards homosexual love were condemned and often connected to other anti-social behavior: a man who questioned the war and espoused pacifism, for example, was labeled a "degenerate," a common term for someone who expressed homosexual behavior. Pacifism and homosexuality become linked in the public consciousness as unacceptable, while serving one's country, comradeship, and heterosexuality are acceptable. Rivers's concern about Sassoon's future, then, is warranted: advocating suppression rather than discussion, Rivers urges Sassoon not to espouse his pacificist views too widely in London, where Sassoon is known as a friend of Robert Ross, who in turn was a friend of Oscar Wilde. The risk of Sassoon's pacifism being used to discredit and "out" him is too great.

The mention of Oscar Wilde's name is a much more typical introduction of homosexuality into the novel's narrative than the direct conversation between Rivers and Sassoon described above. Indeed, that conversation can only occur after a series of more careful, veiled comments on both sides. Whether Rivers believes from their first meeting that Sassoon may be homosexual is not clear. However, Rivers is acutely aware that, in asking Sassoon to discuss the pacifism of Edward Carpenter, "he'd led Sassoon unwittingly on to rather intimate territory" (53). Rivers immediately looks "for a way of redirecting the conversation," but Sassoon takes the risk of introducing Carpenter's *The Intermediate Sex* (1908) into their conversation, of admitting that its thesis "saved" his life, and of asking Rivers what he makes of Carpenter's arguments about a third, or "intermediate," sex (53–54). Rivers provides enough assurance to Sassoon that they can later joke about his sexual preferences, as Rivers fills out Sassoon's admission report:

"I don't include any . . . intimate details."

"Probably just as well. My intimate details disqualify from military service."

Rivers looked up and smiled. "I know." (70–71)

Outside the bounds of their growing friendship and the doctor/patient relationship, Sassoon finds his situation much more tricky. The familiarity between Sassoon and Robert Graves could be read as homosocial with tendencies towards the homosexual, but Graves's parting words to Sassoon firmly demarcate the difference in order to preserve their public personas. After learning that a friend, Peter, had been arrested for soliciting young men outside the local barracks, Graves announces to Sassoon: "It's only fair to tell you that . . . since that happened my affections have been running in more normal channels. I've been writing to a girl called Nancy Nicolson. [. . .] The . . . the only reason I'm telling you this is . . . I'd hate you to have any misconceptions. About me. I'd hate for you to think I was homosexual even in thought. Even if it went no further" (199). Relying on ellipses, Graves talks around the topic of his own sexual preferences, leaving gaps to be filled by his listener's knowledge; only when he offers an outright denial can he speak the word "homosexual."

Men's fear of being read as homosexual or sexually deviant recurs throughout *Regeneration*, either through references to Freud or through jokes. When Anderson tells Rivers about his dream, Anderson becomes acutely self-conscious of its details: his nudity in front of his wife and her friends, being tied up in a straitjacket made from a lady's corset, and the presence of a snake. When Rivers asks if he often dreams about snakes, Anderson agrees and then bursts out: "Well, go on, then [. . .] That's what you Freudian Johnnies are on about all the time, isn't it? Nudity, snakes, *corsets*. You might at least try to look *grateful*, Rivers. It's a gift" (29). Only able to read sexual deviance into his dream, Anderson overlooks another referent for the phallic snake: the one that twines itself on the caduceus badge of the RAMC, whose presence suggests that Anderson's dream has more to do with his relationship to medicine than various sexual practices. Anderson's fear of Freudian meanings, even if they are "derived mainly from secondary or prejudiced sources" as Rivers suspects (31), highlights his concerns about acting correctly and expressing the appropriate desires.

Billy Prior's sexual jokes and innuendoes express not so much his fear of feeling inappropriate desire, but his knowledge that such desire—that showing any sexual desire—is deemed socially inappropriate.[10] Though Prior is decidedly heterosexual in *Regeneration*, the fact that he is decidedly bi-sexual in *The Eye in the Door* and *The Ghost Road* makes his quips and comments in *Regeneration* significant for our understanding of his later character as much as for his character in *Regeneration*. Sexual humor becomes one of his weapons in his battle for control of the doctor/patient relationship, but he underestimates his opponent, since Rivers is hardly fazed by Prior crossing that particular social line. Prior's jokes are usually one-liners that play off of his experiences, putting those experiences into a homosexual or heterosexual context. As he and Rivers piece together his fragmented memories to pinpoint the missing days, they have the following exchange:

"But on that occasion no trouble with the voice? Fourteen days later you were back in the line. Fully recovered?"

"I'd stopped doing the can-can, if that's what you mean."

"Were there any remaining symptoms?"

"Headaches." He watched Rivers makes a note. "It's hardly a reason to stay out of the trenches, is it? *'Not tonight, Wilhelm, I've got a headache'*?" (50)

Using Rivers as his straight man, Prior stages a vaudeville-esque routine to dispel his fears about what might lie forgotten in his memory and to preempt Rivers's control of the conversation. Prior casts himself in the "feminine" role in these two jokes, but his other comments can be charged with a less specific sexual meaning: his description of an attack as feeling *"sexy,"* for instance, when he is pushed by Rivers to recognize the emotional force of the event (78). Aligning sex with death, fear, and terror, Prior's comments acknowledge the force of sexuality but without re-inscribing the culturally sanctioned channels for its power. He inadvertently gives voice to Freud's later theories about the relationship between love *(Eros)* and death *(Thanatos)* by refusing to sidestep the role of sex in his perception of the war. His methods also reveal his own insecurities. Unlike Sassoon's careful phrasing and Graves's ellipses, unlike Anderson's fearful interpretations of his dreams, Prior purposefully includes homosexual desire in his conversation in order to mask other concerns.

THE MORE THINGS CHANGE . . .

The more things change, the more they stay the same: this well-worn phrase captures the lives of the female characters in *Regener-*

ation. Though the war offers them a degree of financial and social freedom unimaginable in the pre-war days, Barker emphasizes how the working class women of the novel are nonetheless trapped by cultural conventions of gender and class. Trespassing upon a decidedly male world, they are expected to be masculine *and* feminine to succeed—and they must be ready to cede their new freedoms when the war is over. Knowing these restrictions does not make their lives any easier, but this knowledge certainly urges them to enjoy what they have for the present moment as fully as possible.

Most of the women of *Regeneration* are of the type we meet in Barker's earlier fiction: hard-working, determined Northerners whose coarse tongues tell the truth about life without compunction. They have also suffered at the hands of their husbands and lovers, and they are consequently relieved to know that those men are now fighting in the trenches rather than in the home. "Do you know what happened on August 4th 1914?" Lizzie asks the unattached Sarah Lumb. Before Sarah can reply, Lizzie answers her own question: "I'll tell you what happened. *Peace* broke out. The only little bit of peace I've ever had. No, I don't want him back. I don't want him back on leave. I don't want him back when it's over. As far as I'm concerned the Kaiser can keep him" (110). Such virulence strikes Sarah as hard-hearted, given what men experience at the front, but Betty's comments put his present experience of war alongside Lizzie's past experience of married life:

You know when I was a kid we used to live next door to them, and it was thump thump thump half the bloody night, you'd've thought she was coming through the wall. Oh, and you used to see her in the yard next morning, and her face'd be all swelled up. "I fell over the coal scuttle," she used to say. Well that used to get me Mam. "*He* knocks you about," she says, "and *you* go round apologizing for it," she says. "Where's the justice in that?" And mind you, she was right, you know. (111)

The historical context that Betty offers for Lizzie's whole-hearted banishment of her husband to the Germans speaks to Lizzie's long-repressed anger and shame. The war not only allows Lizzie's physical separation from an abusive husband, but the emotional opportunity to acknowledge her hatred of him. He may come back, he may even take up his prewar habits, but at least Lizzie has had a taste of what life could be like outside a cycle of spousal abuse.

Lizzie, Betty, and the other women whom Sarah meets while working in the munitions factory are able to earn more money in their war work then they could earn in "respectable" occupations before the war. In terms of social class, Sarah has taken a step down from her previous job as a lady's maid ("ten bob a week") when she and Betty decide to turn to factory work, making bombs in twelve-hour shifts for six days a week ("fifty bob a week"). For Sarah, the slip in social status is worth the extra money (93, 89). Ada Lumb, Sarah's mother, makes the most of the business opportunities the war provides, turning a boating lake ticket office into a cafe to sell tea to young soldiers. Hearing that her mother is charging five pence a cup, Sarah announces, "You're a war profiteer you are, Mam" (196). Ada has her eyes set on even bigger profits ("soup and all sorts, especially with winter coming on"), if she only had the capital at hand (196). After years of scrimping and saving, Ada can enjoy some degree of financial security, but she knows that she will never be able to achieve as much as she would like. As she knows all too well, "You need money to make money" (196), and her economic status holds her back.

The fact that Ada Lumb is not pleased with Sarah's change of employment speaks to the cultural limitations on some working women's new-found financial freedom. Wishing her daughter had stayed a lady's maid, she is troubled by the class of women Sarah meets at the factory: "I'm not saying they're not good sorts—some of them—but you got to admit, Sarah, they're *rough*" (194). She is also displeased with Sarah's bright yellow appearance, another consequence of her munitions work with phosphorus. Aware that appearance signals class affiliation, Ada took pains to instill "[p]rettiness, pliability — at least the appearance of it — all the arts of pleasing" in her two daughters as they were growing up, so they could be widows of young men with good incomes if not their wives (195). While Sarah's sister, Cynthia, dutifully married a young recruit and promptly became a widow, Sarah resisted such a life and struck out on her own. However, other aspects of social respectability are still very much a part of her life: a landlady who forbids men inside the house and expects her in by a decent hour, a feminine appearance (shoes and stockings, hair coiffed) for her night off, and a concerted effort not to appear sexually promiscuous. Even if women were much more likely to have and initiate sexual encounters during wartime, they must still avoid any evidence of such activity. Betty's botched abortion illustrates such concerns, but so, too, does Sarah's decision not to have sex with Billy Prior the first night they met, and her mother's warning to Sarah that Sarah must "put a value on herself": "You'll never gunna get engaged till you learn to keep your knees together. [. . .] No man likes to think that he's sliding in on another man's leavings" (194). Sarah laughs at her mother turn of phrase, but she has already shown herself to be aware of her mother's meaning. That Sarah's mother expects her to marry sooner rather than later is yet another sign that women are bound by pre-war gender roles, rather than free of them.

When he is with Sarah, Billy Prior realizes he feels "out of touch with women": "They seem to have expanded in all kinds of ways, whereas men over the same period had shrunk into a smaller and smaller space" (90). Yet the *women's* experiences contradict Prior's suggestion that there has been a simple reversal of fortunes. If women have "expanded," that expansion has only occurred in a few areas of society: choice of occupation, increased wages, and some freedom from the obligatory domestic duties of a wife and possibly a daughter. In many areas — class, sexual activity, reproduction, appearance — women's lives are just as constricted by prewar gender roles. Major Huntley's diatribe to Rivers about women's reproductive capacities in wartime illustrates how women of all classes are fenced in by biology and its attendant social roles: "Did Rivers know that private soldiers were on average *five inches* shorter than their officers? And yet it was often the better type of woman who chose to limit the size of her family, while her feckless sisters bred the Empire to destruction" (211). Amazingly classist, Major Huntley's "theories on how the women of Britain might be brought back to a proper sense of their duties" indicate that reproduction still determined the scope of most women's lives, especially when those lives are evaluated by men with power. In light of such views, Madge's prophecy rightly keeps the working women's spirits in check: even their bit of freedom is "too good to last" (110). They have no guarantee this modest expansion will remain in place after the war. Madge's comment acknowledges that until men's views of women change permanently, women's experiences in society will remain the same. Allowed to stray into a male preserve for the sake of the war, women of all classes are still expected to toe the line of socialized gender roles to survive.

Billy Prior's complicated view of Sarah exemplifies women's multiple, often contradictory roles during the war, but his character's confusion also suggests that some productive change might develop in the future. For Prior, Sarah is alternately "one of the boys," an ignorant civilian, or a female and feminine space completely separate from all worldly pain. When Sarah and Prior are talking together about the hypocrisy of the officer class, Prior admires Sarah and appreciates her disgust at what he partially represents. In this role, she also represents a link to his own working-class past that he has had to reject in order to succeed as an officer. Yet when they are out amongst the "pleasure seeking crowds" at the beach, Prior can only think of Sarah as separate from him, as representative of the society that created but stays aloof from the war. At such times, he "both envied and despised her, and was quite coldly determined to *get* her. They owed him something, all of them, and she should pay" (128). Since she is a civilian woman and not in the trenches, he aligns her with all who unjustly escape that horror, and he wants to punish them by having sex with her. She becomes a mere object for his purposes of revenge, much as she is reduced to her appearance as a "pretty girl" and forced to "play the role of Medusa" when she stumbles into a ward of severely damaged soldiers at the hospital (160). Most importantly, though, for all her work on munitions, Sarah represents for Prior that which is not war and not society, a space to which he can retreat to escape his experiences. When images from the war flash into his mind while they are together — "the shovel, the sack, the scattered lime," "the eyeball" — Prior decides:

She would never know, because he would never tell her. Somehow if she'd known the worst parts, she couldn't have gone on being a haven for him. He was groping for an idea he couldn't quite grasp. Men said they didn't tell their women about France because they didn't want to worry them. But it was more than that. He needed her ignorance to hide in. (216)

Here, Prior maintains a long-standing tradition which flourished in nineteenth-century Britain and America: an ideology of separate spheres. As best-selling nineteenth-century British author Sarah Stickney Ellis explains, "when the snares of the world" circle around a man, he has only to think of the "humble monitress," his wife, who sits "guarding the fireplace comforts of his distant home," so that her "moral beauty" dispels "the clouds before his mental vision."[11] A woman's "moral beauty" therefore depends on her *not* knowing about the dangers and difficulties attendant on men's lives outside the home: her "ignorance," as Prior imagines, provides him a safe "haven" from the trials of the war.

If Prior's comment stopped here, he would simply replicate a persistent ideology of gender difference and become another Marlow from Conrad's *Heart of Darkness*, who believes European women should be "out of it—completely,"[12] kept separate in all ways from the social and psychological horrors of men's experiences. Instead, Barker has Prior realize the dangers of this desire—how the fulfillment of this desire would place a barrier between the two of them. One part of him wants Sarah to be separate from the realities of his world, "[y]et, at the same time, he wanted to know and be known as deeply as possible. And the two desires were irreconcilable" (216). Through the characters of Sarah Lumb and Billy Prior, Barker shows not an unrealistic liberation of women and men from repressive social norms of gender, but instead one man's first realistic steps towards re-thinking the roles women can play in men's personal and public lives.

"HE SHOULD HAVE STUCK WITH HIS OWN"

Though different in many respects, Rivers and Prior share the ability to see at least two sides to their culture's dominant beliefs. Rivers's ability is typically expressed through his capacity for empathy and his knowledge of other cultures, while Prior's ability takes more tendencious forms, evolving from his multiple experiences within British culture. One of Rivers's blind spots, however, is class, as his conversations and interactions with Prior and Sassoon reveal. Although both are Second-Lieutenants, Rivers treats Prior and Sassoon differently, revealing his own class prejudices. Since Prior has not, like Sassoon, "stuck with his own" (57), Prior straddles the line between working class and upper-class culture as one of the war's many "temporary gentlemen." "[N]either fish nor fowl," in his father's words, Prior makes the most of his liminal status in order to reveal class ideologies not only as socially determined (rather than natural), but also as pitifully out of touch and dangerous for all concerned. Prior's ability to "pass" for upper- or working-class grants him a pass into otherwise unspoken territories of his culture.

Perhaps because Sassoon is never really diagnosed as "ill," perhaps because his pre-war life of hunting, cricket, and writing poetry echoes a world of leisure familiar to (if not shared by) Rivers, perhaps because Sassoon associates with members of the aristocracy—perhaps for such reasons, "Second-Lieutenant Sassoon" soon becomes "Siegfried" during his appointments with Rivers, and the formalities attendant on Rivers's relationships with his other patients disappear during his growing friendship with Sassoon. Indeed, before long, Rivers offers to put Sassoon up for membership at his club, the Conservative Club, so he has "an alternative base" (70). By contrast, "Second-Lieutenant Prior" remains "Mr Prior" for the duration of his stay at Craiglockhart. Rivers's initial impression of Prior as a "thin, fair-haired young man of twenty-two with high cheekbones, a short, blunt nose and a supercilious expression" (41) morphs into something much more class-based when he hears Prior's voice for the first time: "A Northern accent, not ungrammatical, but with the vowel sounds distinctly flattened, and the faintest trace of sibilance. Hearing Prior's voice for the first time had the curious effect of making Prior look different. Thinner, more defensive. And, at the same time, a lot tougher" (49). Inflected by his knowledge of Prior's Northern origins and combative demeanor, Prior becomes a "little, spitting, sharp-boned alley cat" in officer's clothing (49)—a decidedly different species than the other Second-Lieutenant in his care whose good looks attract "admiring glances" from both men and women (5).[13]

In his conversations with Prior, Rivers introduces the issue of class in a covert way, but Prior refuses to maintain a discreet relationship to this defining feature of British society. Prior forces Rivers to see its role at Craiglockhart as well as on the front lines, implicating Rivers in replicating the unspoken privileges of class. When pressed by Prior to ask a specific question about Prior's experience in France, Rivers asks how Prior "fit in," with the following results:

Prior's face shut tight. "You mean, did I encounter any snobbery?"
"Yes."
"Not more than I have here."
Their eyes locked. Rivers said, "But you did encounter it?"
"Yes. It's made perfectly clear when you arrive that some people are more welcome than others. It helps if you've been to the right school. It helps if you hunt, it helps if your shirts are the right colour. Which is a *deep* shade of khaki, by the way."
In spite of himself, Rivers looked down at his shirt.
"Borderline," said Prior.
"And yours?"
"Not borderline. Nowhere near." (66)

Unwilling to separate his experiences of snobbery on the front lines with his experiences of it at Craiglockhart, Prior asks Rivers to remember that the position of doctor does not remove his class privilege. Prior's tactics in this exchange seek to disrupt the doctor/ patient relationship, as he does in other instances, only this time he uses Rivers's "borderline" khaki to force Rivers to acknowledge his own class insecurities, as Rivers looks at his shirt "in spite of himself."

By admitting to his working class origins, Prior is free to move between his personas of upper class officer and working class "alley cat" for the rest of their conversation. On the one hand, he acknowledges that he was "in love" once with the patriotic glory captured in verse by poets like Tennyson in "The Charge of the Light Brigade" and that he excelled in most "upper-class" tasks he was called upon to perform. On the other hand, he emphasizes the absurdity of official practices such as "the Seat," of unreasonable and foolhardy field punishments, and of the perception that their attacks on the Germans would somehow end in "one big glorious *cavalry charge*" (66). Most importantly, Prior wishes to rid those on the home front of the myth that class does not matter at the front: "Ballocks. What you wear, what you eat. Where you sleep. What you carry" — even what quality of sex you are able to purchase for your money (67). Mimicking the "mock public school voice" (131) in alternation with a colloquial vocabulary more suited to the North, Prior defies allegiance to only one class, disrupting his listeners' relationship to him and their own invisible class connections. Nonetheless, Prior wants to go back to the front because he knows that such war service will qualify him for "the Club to end all clubs" (135). His status as an officer will only be valuable if he can enact that crucial component, securing his footing on the upper-class side of his divided class identity.

Just as Billy Prior's indeterminate class status provides him with perspective on class, so too does the working class perspective of Sarah and her friends at the factory. For the working class women, the *upper class* signals degeneracy, rather than the other way around. Speaking from her experience of working for an upper class family, Madge relates that the "biggest part" of upper class men are homosexuals, including the son of the family she worked for: "But you know he had no sisters, so he never met lasses that way. Goes to school, no lasses. Goes to university — no lasses. Time he finally claps eyes on me, it's too late, isn't it? It's *gelled*. And even the ones that aren't like that, they take one look at the Missus and bugger off round the Club. [. . .] Beats me how they breed" (200). Turning upper-class status into a joke rather than privilege, Madge both finds a target for her anger at the class system and reveals how *unnatural* upper class society is, if natural constitutes heterosexuality. The "honour" emblematic of a gentleman's class undergoes a reversal as well in Sarah's view of officers' hypocrisy. She tells Prior that she is disgusted by the fact that officers censor their soldiers' letters home but their own letters are sealed unread (131). Prior privately agrees with Sarah, but does not voice his opinion.

Interestingly, by the end of the novel, Sassoon and Prior come to a similar view of upper class privilege in the face of war. When Graves tries to argue that Sassoon must keep his word to his country and his men by fulfilling his contract of service, Sassoon rejects the warrant of Graves's claim: that the generals or the soldiers care about honour. Sassoon argues, "the people who're keeping this war going don't give a damn about the 'Bobbies' and the 'Tommies.' And they don't let 'gentlemanly behavior' stand in the way either when it comes to feathering their own nests. [. . .] As for 'bad form' and 'gentlemanly behavior'—that's just suicidal stupidity" (199). For both Sassoon and Prior, upper class privilege is a smoke screen for actions that result in needless death and wasted energies on the battlefield and unwarranted control at home. Whereas Sassoon is ready to retreat from his class privilege into untimely death on the battlefield, however, Prior is ready to work his for all it is worth.

THE POWER OF THE IMAGINATION

Though it is easy to overlook the word's presence in Sassoon's "Declaration," "imagination" plays an important role in Sassoon's indictment of continued hostilities. He concludes with the hope that his words "may help to destroy the callous complacence with which the majority of those at home regard the continuance of agonies which they do not share, and which they have not sufficient imagination to realize" (3). Castigated for a failure of imagination, the public continues down a path prescribed by others, unable or unwilling to pretend that war may be other than "official" publications suggest, regardless of what soldiers say when they return from the trenches. In *Regeneration* as a whole, the imagination plays a more ambivalent role. It is the source of pain, both physical and emotional, yet it is also the source of empathy, of healing, and of art.

When Sassoon asks the public to make use of their imagination, he is asking them to imagine the horrors of the war, to conceive monstrous images, in order to comprehend its destructive force. Other characters also ponder the use of the imagination in such ways, if for quite different ends. Prior remembers the "power" that No Man's Land had over his imagination: what by day "shrank to a small, pock-marked stretch of ground" grew to an "immensity" at night, something beyond comprehension (214). Its horror became boundless, inhuman. Owen describes a similar experience of his imagination, as he sat in a trench whose sides were full of skulls. It was somehow "easier to believe they were men from Marlborough's army" than men killed just a few years before, Owen tells Sassoon: "It's as if all other wars had somehow . . . distilled themselves into this war, and that makes it something you . . . almost can't challenge" (83). Likewise, Burns, another of Rivers's patients and one whose trauma nearly exceeds belief, ponders the dark force of the imagination. Asking Rivers, "Do you know what Christ died of?" and nodding to Rivers's response — "Suffocation" — Burns continues,

That's what I find so horrifying. Somebody had to *imagine* that death. I mean, just in order to invent it as a method for execution. Do you know that thing in the Bible? "The imagination of man's heart is evil from his youth"? I used to wonder why pick on that? Why his *imagination*? But it's absolutely right. (183)

In identifying such methods of execution, the mortality of the trenches, and the power of No Man's Land as the result of the imagination, Barker asks us to remember that the war itself is the result of human effort, of the human mind. To locate the imagination in the realm of the human means to locate it within the realm of human control. If it is possible for a society to imagine ways of killing, it must be possible for a society to imagine ways to stop or prevent killing. It must be possible for "the imagination of man's heart" to work for good as well as evil.

To emphasize how imagination can work for good, Barker offers us several instances of its more benevolent results. Not only does Rivers's capacity for empathy rely upon his imaginative engagement with his patients' experiences, but his method of treatment depends upon his patients' ability to remember — an act which involves an imaginative recreation of past events. The imagination works to heal the mind here, rather than crippling it. In turn, Sassoon's poetry becomes, in Rivers's terms, a "therapeutic" act: "Sassoon's determination to remember might well account for his early and rapid recovery [. . . .] He thought that Sassoon's poetry and his protest sprang from a single source, and each could be linked to his recovery from that terrible period of nightmares and hallucinations" (26). Determined to remember so he can transmute his experience into art, Sassoon's poetry shows the imaginative powers of the mind at work for constructive ends — for his benefit and for the benefit of others.

The collaborative efforts of Sassoon and Owen further illustrate the benefits of the imagination, where one mind helps another communicate with an audience of readers. Their collaboration also dismisses the Romantic vision of the artist who works only in isolation. The imaginative acts of remembering and artistic creation become instead a collaborative task. Playing audience for each other, Sassoon and Owen struggle to find the right words to communicate their emotional experiences and responses to the war. If in some ways the war has emptied language of its power—"Language runs out on you, in the end, the names [of Mons, Loos, Ypres, the Somme, Arras] were left to say it all," Prior thinks (90)—Sassoon and Owen look for ways to make words communicate meaning in new ways. As they workshop Owen's poem "Anthem for Doomed Youth," for example, they search for new combinations: "passing bells" for "minute-bells," "the guns" for "our guns" (141). Sassoon also convinces Owen that art cannot easily be separated from life, as Owen first suggests (84–5). For Sassoon, art cannot serve humanity to the best of its imaginative abilities if it does not interact with human life, however horrific or beautiful that life may be.

LIFE INTO ART, ART INTO LIFE

The poetry of Siegfried Sassoon and Wilfred Owen helps readers to have "sufficient imagination" to realize the horror of war in order to prevent its continuation or recurrence. So, too, does Pat Barker's *Regeneration*. Based in part on historical events, Barker's skillful blending of fact and fiction, of science and literature, not only raises questions about how to imagine World War I, but also about the relationship between story and history and about the right of the novelist to (re)write history for her readers. Barker's choice of form, style, and material sets *Regeneration* apart from other modern novels about the Great War and earns it a place in a growing popular canon of contemporary historical fiction.

Published in 1991, *Regeneration* appeared in British bookstores in the company of a number of novels that looked to history to understand the past and the present: Peter Ackroyd's *Chatterton*, Martin Amis's *Time's Arrow*, Julian Barnes's *A History of the World in 10½ Chapters*, A. S. Byatt's *Possession*, Kazuo Ishiguro's *The Remains of the Day*, Salman Rushdie's *Satanic Verses*, Rose Tremain's *Restoration*, and Jeanette Winterson's *The Passion* are but a few that fill this category. A number of these authors also chose to take historical figures and events as the frame for their story's characters and plot. In collapsing or blurring the boundaries between fact and fiction, such authors often ask their readers to question our cultural ideas of history: Who decides what story receives the official label of "history"? How much difference is there (or, should there be) between a story and history? What is missing from the official historical narrative that can help us better understand who those people were and who we are now? Of course, these questions are not new ones to literature—Jane Austen's Catherine Moreland poses similar ones to Henry Tilney in *Northanger Abbey*—but the 1980s and 1990s saw a marked increase in fiction with these goals, in contrast to the fiction of the 1950s and 1960s, which typically took the pulse of the present by representing the present moment.

To use historical figures for some or all of a novel's characters has several results.[14] First, their presence in the narrative can make the story seem more "real," more connected to the world of the reader. Their presence also signals to the reader that there is another "story," another "history," that exists for the historical figures which their fictional counterparts can provide or enact. The degree to which an author makes us aware of the relationship between the "real" historical person and the "fictional" character will undoubtedly affect our reading experience and our perception of the novel's themes. The form of the narrative itself will likely signal how "aware" we are to be. So, whereas Salman Rushdie presents the narrative of *Satanic Verses* in a way that makes us extraordinarily conscious of how it is put together (addressing the reader directly, playing with the visual and aural texture of words), Pat Barker does not draw our attention to the way *Regeneration* is constructed. While some authors prefer to emphasize the act of historical appropriation, Barker does not do so in *Regeneration*. Instead, she relies on her readers' familiarity or lack of familiarity with the history of Sassoon's and Owen's visit to Craiglockhart War Hospital in 1917 to meet Dr. W. H. R. Rivers. She does provide some historical information to tell us who is "real" and who must be, by contrast, "made up," but she offers this information in an "Author's Note" at the *end* of the novel, rather than at the beginning.

In a way, the textual presence of Sassoon and Owen through their quoted poetry makes the narrative of *Regeneration* feel more "real" than any knowledge we have about their lives. Whereas we may not know much about Sassoon or Owen *as men*, we are fairly likely to have encountered one of their poems in our lives, either in an anthology of poetry, in school, or during some public event on Memorial Day or Remembrance Day. As historical figures, then, Sassoon and Owen are important to Barker's retelling of history for the meanings their poetry has accrued as much as for who Siegfried Sassoon and Wilfred Owen were. Barker does make use of their lives, particularly Owen's life, as she crafts her novel, just as she makes use of Rivers's case studies to create fictional characters like Burns and Anderson (Perry, *Backtalk*, 1993, 52–3). Indeed, there are many similarities between the wartime experiences of Billy Prior and those of Wilfred Owen in particular. Like Owen, Prior suffers a breakdown in 1917 after a series of events, and he experienced a traumatic siege in No Man's Land as he and his platoon held down a position for fifty hours. However, these "real life" details become part of the larger picture of war the novel presents, instead of a retelling of Sassoon's or Owen's lives in 1917.[15]

In her approach to those questions about the relationship between "history" and "story," then, Barker is interested in creating a psychologically realistic story to complement history, a story where the focus is on the emotional states of the characters. Point of view plays an important role in creating this realism. During the narrative of *Regeneration*, we are always aligned with a character's point of view. This point of view shifts between characters during the course of the novel — from Rivers to Sassoon, and then back to Rivers during chapter 1, for instance — but we always stay connected to one of the character's experiences. In selecting this method of free indirect style (*style indirect libre*), Barker brings us close to the characters' emotions while still maintaining some degree of distance or perspective. Her method differs from the ironic distance that results from a more omniscient third person narrative voice or a narrative voice that shifts between third and second person to address the reader directly. Barker's choice of form is important, because the characters's emotional experiences are the plot of the novel. The novel's form therefore emphasizes where our focus should be. As a result, we also do not encounter detailed descriptions of characters' surroundings, clothing, or personal belongings. Instead, certain physical details are singled out as representative of characters' actions or experiences: Sarah's yellow skin, Rivers's rubbing his eyes, Sassoon tugging at the thread on his uniform where the Military Cross was once pinned. We never learn what the interior of Craiglockhart looks like, but we do know that the patients do not have locks on their doors. That one detail — their lack of privacy — tells us quite a bit about Craiglockhart's influence on its inhabitants's emotional states.

The characteristics noted so far for *Regeneration* contribute to its unusual place in a canon of war literature. Add to them Barker's decision to select one small slice of time (July to November of 1917) and a place *not* situated near the front and its trenches

(Craiglockhart War Hospital in Edinburgh, Scotland), and we have arrived at quite a different formula for the war novel. The war lurks in the narrative of *Regeneration*, just as it lurks in the memories of the men at Craiglockhart, surfacing at certain moments while never fully out of mind. Unlike a usual war novel, such as Remarque's *All Quiet on the Western Front*, we do not ever go to the front with *Regeneration*'s characters or experience a bombardment during the present time of the novel's narrative. Instead, we remain with them within the safety of Craiglockhart War Hospital, and the violence and the terror of the war happen offstage, much as violence does in Greek drama. However, just as in Greek drama, the fact that graphic death does not happen in front of us does not mean the memories or stories of those who have seen it will not be horrifying. In fact, the retelling might be even worse, since it relies upon the imagination of the audience to re-create the scene. Indeed, Barker relies on the "imagination of the [reader's] heart" (183) to fill in the gaps left open by patients' narratives, according to her narrative cues. *Regeneration* does not seek to provide the epic scope and the close detail of trench warfare that is the call to remembrance in Sebastian Faulks's *Birdsong* (1992). It does not link war to a rupture in natural law, as Faulks's narrative suggests, a rupture only reparable by physical rebirth. Instead, *Regeneration* asks readers to consider remembering as a form of healing, as a way to regenerate the bodies and the minds damaged by the body politic. By locating the war's sins in the laws of society rather than the laws of nature, Barker offers a method of healing available not just to the Lost Generation, but to contemporary ones.

3

The Novel's Reception

Regeneration was well-received by reviewers in both the UK and the United States. Criticism, when it occurred, was in the minority and couched inside praise. The range of publications which have reviewed *Regeneration* — from daily newspapers to medical journals like *The Lancet* and medical databases — further indicates its widespread appeal.

Barker's ability to blend fact and fiction, her characterization, and her style are valued by reviewers in the UK and the United States. Peter Kemp, writing for the *Sunday Times*, admires how Barker can present so much trauma "without a tremor of sensationalism or sentimentality," a point also noted by Michael Upchurch in *The Seattle Times*: "Barker's prose has a clipped intensity that handily accommodates hallucination, dry wit and sticky points of honor." Kemp also notes how her ability to create compelling individual characters wards off any chance that sections of the book could "flatten into a thesis." Michael Harris of the *Los Angeles Times* casts Barker as a doctor herself, as she "skillfully sutures together fact and fiction," making her characters "complex and credible." For Herbert Mitgang of the *New York Times*, Barker's fictional additions to the historical text are "informed invention" and worthy of praise. "Brave" and "ambitious" in its approach to war, Barker's novel succeeds for Justine Picardie because of the compassion and optimism portrayed in Rivers's character. Paul Taylor, writing for *The Independent,* believes *Regeneration* offers a "warm, humane portrait" in Rivers which compensates for any failings.

Those reviewers who do note failings in *Regeneration* question Barker's realism (in his review for the *TLS,* for instance, Ben Shephard notes some anachronistic phrases) and Barker's decision to end her novel not with the end of the war, but with Sassoon on his way back to France. "Why there, when the rest of the historical story is so dramatic and moving?" asks Samuel Hynes, historian and reviewer for the *New York Times,* "Why not follow Sassoon to the front, where he fought again until he was wounded by one of his own men and was evacuated to England?" Though Hynes answers his own questions—"Because, Ms. Barker would no doubt reply, her interest was in Dottyville, not in France"—Hynes still believes there is a "narrative cost in stopping where she does, short of the story's natural closure." Several other reviewers, Jackie Wullschlager and Kevin Ray for instance, feel that the novel lacks depth in its historical development and characterization, so that, as Ray says, we watch it "falling away from itself as fiction, flickering, even in the page, somewhere between fiction and film." Wullschlager's language is more blunt: the quotations from the poems and some explanatory dialogue "recall a stagey war film." Wullschlager also feels that Barker weakens her work by having the action "caged in a distinct time and place, whose period feel, as in almost any historical novel, is inauthentic." Paul Taylor picks up on the tendency Wullschlager notes for explanatory dialogue in his criticisms: "The discussions in which Sassoon helps his fellow-patient Wilfred Owen with his poetry sound a bit like a programme for the Open University." Nonetheless, Taylor, like others who criticize elements of the novel, concludes with praise for the themes Barker's novel conveys.

The publication of *Regeneration* had an interesting effect on the press's view of Barker as a woman writer. Most reviewers on both sides of the Atlantic were surprised at the book's plot, seeing little similarity between her earlier fiction about working class women and a novel that focused on mainly upper-class men and war.[16] Many also seemed to forget that Barker had already taken a male point of view in *Liza's England* and *The Man Who Wasn't There* and that she did not only write about women. For some reviewers, like Philip Hensher of the *Guardian*, *Regeneration* and the subsequent volumes of the trilogy redeemed Barker from a downward spiral, so that she becomes "a rare example of an author who has drastically, and successfully changed course." If, as Hensher says, "some worrying questions began to surface about her range" — "more tight-knit working class communities; more faulty dialogue" — *Regeneration* put such fears to rest. "Of course, there's nothing wrong with going on writing about the same communities," Hensher adds, but Barker's change of course shows that she is no longer "managing to prove a point only by limiting her subject matter." For Justine Picardie, writing for *The Independent*, *Regeneration* "comes as a surprise," given Barker's earlier fiction. Claiming that the result is "an austere and very fine novel," Picardie concludes, "One might say that Pat Barker has herself emerged from a kind of chrysalis, from the ghetto of being a 'women's writer,' perhaps?" Like Hensher, Picardie suggests that Barker's shift in material has placed her in a more exaulted, lauded, and developed category as a writer; its publication allows her to attain a new, if rightly earned, place at the best part of town rather than in the "ghetto" of women's writing.

However, a few reviewers — joined by more by the time *The Ghost Road* had appeared — did see clear connections between Bar-

ker's earlier and current fiction. Candice Rodd begins her review
by acknowledging that "you could almost be forgiven for thinking
there are two Pat Barkers," but her review proceeds to dismantle
such a perception. Claudia Roth Pierpoint offers an interesting
analysis of Barker's shift in her review of *The Ghost Road:* "The
author has certainly proved that she can 'do men,' but her real tour
de force may lie in having reinvented herself while retaining all the
vigor of her old unrespectable themes. This war trilogy is as feminist
and as class-embattled a work as Pat Barker has ever written." Pierpoint's choice of words — "reinvent herself" — is nonetheless telling
and harkens back to the first reviews which claimed Barker had
transformed herself by selecting a new venue for her talents. One
wonders if comments like Hensher's are the consequence of a
gendered perspective on what constitutes the appropriate subject
matter for "good writing." Claudia Roth Pierpoint remarks how in
England "much has been made of the perception that the book
could easily be taken for the work of a man, and that this should be
viewed as a kind of triumph." Pierpoint links such views to Barker's
choice of style, particularly her "ruttingly unromantic" descriptions
of sex, and Picardie reminds her readers that such qualities were
duly present in Barker's first two novels, "which might also have
been characterized as masculine if not for the fact they were about
the lives of poor and desperate women."

By being judged according to content rather than style, Barker
gains entry to the (male) canon of British literature. No longer
"ignored by other branches of the press," as Barker of Virago rue-
fully remarks to Donna Perry ("Going Home"), the publication of
all three novels of the *Regeneration* trilogy has allowed Barker of
Viking to become, in the words of the *Guardian*, "one of the
strongest and most interesting novelists of her generation" (Stoffman, 1998).

4

The Novel's Performance

Regeneration has achieved record sales during the past ten years on both sides of the Atlantic, but particularly in the UK (Wilson). Sales rose further in the UK when *Regeneration* was republished with *The Eye in the Door* and *The Ghost Road* as *The Regeneration Trilogy* in 1996 after Barker won the Booker Prize.[17] Aside from a spot of legal trouble from George Sassoon, Siegfried Sassoon's son and literary executor, which seems to have been quickly resolved, Barker has encountered none of the scandals or difficulties some authors experience when they chose historical figures for their fiction.[18] In the United States, *Regeneration* was chosen by the *New York Times* as one of the four best novels of 1992. Max Davidson notes, "Even in the United States, where the First World War did not make such a deep impression on the national psyche, the books have resonated with readers." This interest can be explained in part, Barker says to Davidson, because "[p]eople have picked up on the parallels with the Vietnam war": "The disillusion. The psychic fall-out. The doubts about whether the war was worthwhile."

Reader comments posted to the "Customer Reviews" at Amazon.com speak to the novel's success, giving it 4½ out of 5 stars. Though certainly not representative of all readers, the "Customer Reviews" offer a snap-shot perspective on an international group of readers.[19] These readers were impressed by Barker's abilities to weave fact and fiction into a compelling narrative and praised, as many published reviewers did, the novel's pace and energy. After finishing the novel, many readers decided to learn more about the history of the time, either by reading the war poets themselves or books about the period. Above all, most remarked that *Regeneration* made them think about the war and their relationship to the events the novel depicts: "It is not often that you find a book that actually makes you sit up and think about the message being conveyed by the author," writes Ivan Kinsman from London, England. Ed Kehoe, a combat veteran from New York, says that Barker's depiction of the "horrors of war" was stunning, yet, "as in war, the only redemptive aspects of Barker's book lie in the complex and profound interaction of its characters." Finally, several readers praised the perspective *Regeneration* provided on mental health and the practice of medicine. A reader who identified himself as a physician felt the novel offered "the best depiction of the complexities of the doctor-patient relationship" he has encountered, especially the "moral dilemma inherent in balancing the claims of the state with that of individuals."

Part of the reason for the *British* pubic's embrace of *Regeneration* could be seen as a fortunate confluence of its publication date and an increased interest in the First World War. Arriving on bookshelves in 1991, *Regeneration* was part of the first wave of a renewed focus on war and remembrance, a cultural trend which continued through the 1990s. The popularity of historical novels like the *Regeneration* trilogy joined an explosion of "remembrance": exhibits of war photography, films, documentaries, oral history projects to record the memories of veterans, and fairly elaborate anniversary events to commemorate the beginning and end of the war — all designed to immerse the present British public in a collective past. In light of her novels, Barker was often asked to contribute to such projects. As early as November 1991, just a few months after the publication of *Regeneration*, Barker appeared with poet Sir Stephen Spender and historian Paul Fussell in a series of readings and lectures at the Poetry Society (Davis, 1991). In the years that followed, Barker was often called upon to be a voice for those of the First World War. On 14 May 1996, Barker hosted an episode of the BBC program "The Works," titled "On the Ghost Road"; as mentioned in the biography, on 11 November 2000 Barker presented the Armistice Day programmes for BBC Knowledge (Dickson, 2000). More generally, Barker is frequently asked to comment on the First World War in her interviews, and *Regeneration* has become a reference point for the war, as David Herman's review of Ben Shephard's book from December 2000 indicates: "Mention shell-shock and we think of the First World War: Captain Blackadder pretending to be mad to get out of the trenches; Siegfried Sassoon in Pat Barker's *Regeneration*; even Lord Peter Whimsey who, in *Busman's Holiday*, admits that he 'has never been really right since the war.'"

Both Barker and *Regeneration*, then, have been accorded a daunting responsibility: to represent the war for the current generation, and this responsibility has acquired further difficulties since *Regeneration* was published in 1991. In a 1998 commentary for *The Independent* running under the headline "Do Today's Public Rituals Hinder Our Understanding of War?" historian Niall Ferguson asks, "Has Remembrance become an empty ritual?" Ferguson names Barker as one of the first to "tap into the public's surprisingly long-lived interest in the subject, surprising because so few people are still alive who actually remember the war," while also recognizing that her books were just the beginning of a much more exten-

sive effort to remember. Concluding that such public rituals are a
way to "make the lucky majority mindful of the unlucky few,"
Ferguson worries about a creeping tendency to justify the war in
the "high diction" refuted by Sassoon and Owen. Given Ferguson's
concerns, it would seem the continued popularity of *Regeneration*
and the trilogy at the turn of the twenty-first century is significant.
Regeneration provides a constant check to those "public rituals"
which often serve the very beliefs and values that Barker's characters
question, find lacking, and ultimately reject.

WHO'S READING REGENERATION? EVERYONE.

The popularity of Barker's *Regeneration* is spread across the demo-
graphics of the reading public. Age is but one boundary that has
been crossed. Introduced recently as a text for A-Level exams, many
sixth form students are reading her novel—some happily and some
less happily, according to the "Customer Comments" and "Customer Reviews" posted at the web sites for Amazon.co.uk and
Barnes & Noble.com. *Regeneration* is also on a list complied by the
Librarians at Thurso High School for the "Specialist Study: Literature" in the Scottish Qualification Authority's Higher Level exami-
nation ("Introduction"). Barker's novels are finding their way into
high school curriculums outside of Britain, too: Geoff Sammon
argues for the inclusion of *Regeneration* or *The Eye in the Door* for
Sixth Form classes in Germany's *Oberstusse*, in part to rectify
German mis-perceptions of English culture (43–44).

More telling perhaps than the appearance of Barker's *Regeneration* in high school curricula is its appearance on the bookshelves
of both men and women. According to a survey about the impact
of gender on reading habits (published in March 2000 and sponsored by the Orange Prize organizers), *Regeneration* had the distinc-

tion of being one of three women's novels in the "neutral zone":
Pat Barker's *Regeneration*, Beryl Bainbridge's *Every Man for Himself*
and Ann Michael's *Fugitive Pieces* were all perceived as being "neither male nor female" according to the criteria of the survey. Since
male readers are "unduly influenced by the sex of the author, by
the look of the cover and by the use of emotional words in the
title," Pat Barker's *Regeneration* appears to be a safe choice, a "male
read." Being able to garner the male reading public is a boon: while
women read widely, men are careful to shy away from anything that
might be a "female read." Indeed, the survey showed that *Regeneration* appealed to 62 per cent of men and 48 percent of women
surveyed (Thorpe, 2000; McCartney, 2000). There are certainly
ironies in male readers' embrace of Barker's fifth novel, given Barker's status as a woman writer who wrote for women until the
publication of *Regeneration*. Another would be that, as Barker tells
Donna Perry, "here in Britain men have tended to see this feminist
perspective [in the novel] rather more than the women" (*Backtalk*
52). *Regeneration* has certainly earned Barker an unusual place in
the history of British women's writing, one that continues to flourish
since the publication of *The Eye in the Door* and *The Ghost Road*.

REGENERATION, THE FILM

Though Barker mentions to interviewer Candice Rodd in 1993 that
there would be a BBC television adaptation of *Regeneration* with
Albert Finney as Rivers, this production never materialized. Instead,
we have Gillies MacKinnon's adaptation of *Regeneration* (1997, 113
min.) for the big screen. The film streamlines Barker's complex
novel considerably, choosing to emphasize the theme of father and
son, the betrayal of a younger generation by the older one. Shifting
dialogue so that Rivers presents a much more unified position

against the war and for his role as doctor at the start of the film, the screenplay is able to align Sassoon and Prior against Rivers. Other revisions alter qualities of Barker's novel, yet the resulting film still conveys many of Barker's themes. Indeed, Barker tells her readers at the *Guardian* that "it was [a] relief to be able to say genuinely that I liked it" ("Pat Barker's Answers," 2001).

A joint venture between the UK and Canada, the film was more successful in those two countries than in the States because of distribution and poor timing of its release. The film premiered at the Edinburgh International Film Festival in 1997 and opened the British Renaissance sidebar at Venice Film Festival on 28 August 1997; it also received a Gala screening in Toronto on 8 September 1997 ("Dougray Scott," 2001). General release occurred in the UK on 21 November 1997 (there was a screening on 8 November sponsored by the London Film Festival), but the film was not released for the international public until 1998. (The United States and Canadian release happened on 14 August 1998.) The film stars Jonathan Pryce (*The Age of Innocence, Carrington*) as Dr. William Rivers; James Wilby (*Maurice, Howards End*) as Siegfried Sassoon; Jonny Lee Miller (*Trainspotting, Afterglow, Mansfield Park*) as Billy Prior; Stuart Bunce as Wilfred Owen; Tanya Allen as Sarah; John Neville (*The Fifth Element; The Adventures of Baron Munchausen*) as Dr. Yealland; and Rupert Procter as Burns. Filmed on location in Glasgow and the Clyde Valley in 1996 ("Dougray Scott," 2001) with a screenplay by Allan Scott, the film garnered a number of award nominations: Best British Film (British Academy Awards); Best Director, Best Actor, Film Making the Most of Resources Within a Limited Budget (British Independent Film Award); Best Achievement in Art Direction, in Cinematography, in Costume Design, in Direction, in Editing, Best Motion Picture, Best Music Score, Best Overall Sound, Best Performance by an Actor in a Leading Role, Best Screenplay, Best Sound Editing (Genie

Awards); and nominations in the categories of Expose and Peace (Political Film Society, USA).

The impressive list of nominations followed on the heels of many favorable reviews in the UK and Canadian and some mixed reviews in the United States. While all reviewers tended to praise the opening shot—the camera travels above a muddy battlefield bathed in bluish light, finding the bodies of dead and nearly dead men moaning for relief amidst the wreckage of an assault, "like Stanley Spencer out of Hieronymous Bosch" (Andrews, 1997)—reviews begin to diverge after that point. The reason lies perhaps in the context for each film: UK and Canadian reviewers tended to view and review *Regeneration* favorably alongside another British anti-war film, *Welcome to Saravejo*, while US reviewers had *Saving Private Ryan* already in their heads as they wrote their mixed reviews of *Regeneration*. Writing for *The Observer*, Philip French calls *Regeneration* a "superb film" which Gillies Mackinnon directs "with quiet authority," while Trevor Johnston (*The New Scotsman*) is particularly impressed by what Mackinnon has been able to create on a budget less than £5 million. UK reviewers also noticed what was missing from Allan Scott's screenplay while US reviewers did not. The reviewer for *The Guardian* ("Regeneration Game") warned viewers that they might miss the complexity of Prior's sexuality and the depth of his relationship with Sarah, as did Nigel Andrews for the *Financial Times* and David Gritten for *The Daily Telegraph*. A few UK reviewers questioned the whole endeavor—"It's the curse of British film-making that cinema is viewed not so much a method of storytelling with incidental educational possibilities, as a teaching tool existing purely for our mental and moral improvement," wrote Anne Billson for the *Sunday Telegraph*—but most found praise for the actors' performances and selected elements of the film.

Reviewers in the United States could not seem to shake the echo of Spielberg's opening scene in *Saving Private Ryan* from their eyes or ears. While John Hartl saw the two films as quite similar, so similar that *Regeneration* "plays like a sequel," Kevin Thomas cites another critic who calls *Regeneration* "a cerebral 'Saving Private Ryan.'" Thomas, though, grants the film to be "intelligent" and "well-produced," but Hartl wonders if the screenwriter should have drawn on the other two books of the trilogy. Janet Maslin of *The New York Times* offers the most generous comparison between the two films, acknowledging that *Regeneration* had actually been ready for release before *Saving Private Ryan* and describing it as a "literate, subtly acted film" which is "stirring and articulate." Lloyd Sachs of *The Chicago-Sun Times* provides perhaps the most insightful comparison: "If 'Saving Private Ryan' is a roaring symphony," then "'Regeneration' is a powerfully muted tone poem." Given such reviews, it is not surprising that the film did not stay in U.S. theaters very long; it is even difficult to locate the film on video, either under the title *Regeneration* or *Behind the Lines*, its alternate US title. Copies are readily available in the UK and in Canada.

5

Further Reading and Discussion Questions

OTHER READINGS

Many readers who enjoyed *Regeneration* turn to the next books of the *Regeneration* trilogy: *The Eye in the Door* and *The Ghost Road*. Readers who are fascinated by the fictional Billy Prior are rewarded by Barker's focus on his character in the subsequent books. While both novels continue to follow Rivers and his work with war neuroses and psychological disorders, they also offer an even blunter look at homosexuality and the violence of war, both muted in *Regeneration*. Barker's next novel, *Another World*, will certainly appeal to fans of *Regeneration*, since the novel connects the past of the First World War with late-twentieth century England. *Liza's England*, Barker's third novel, also places the First World War in historical context. Liza's experiences of the war on the home front are an early look at the working women Barker will create for *Regeneration*. The opening to *Regeneration* is also collected in an anthology of twentieth-century literature about the First World War, *The Vintage*

Book of War Stories (1999), edited by Sebastian Faulks and Jorg Hensgen. The selections from this anthology might interest readers of *Regeneration*, providing further context for Barker's novel. Faulks and Hensgen also provide a select bibliography of war writings they considered for the collection but could not include, organized according to the war they describe.

A number of readers who post comments to Amazon.com mention that reading *Regeneration* encouraged them to seek out Barker's original sources. Some readers turn to the work of the war poets themselves, Siegfried Sassoon and Wilfred Owen, as well as Robert Graves. Their poetry, letters, and memoirs form the basis for much of Barker's novel. Other readers turned to Rivers's *Conflict and Dream* or Paul Fussell's landmark study, *The Great War and Modern Memory*, for further historical context. There have been several recent books on the First World War that explore the people and issues Barker raises in her novel, too, such as Ben Shephard's *A War of Nerves: Soldiers and Psychiatrists, 1914–1994* and Niall Ferguson's *The Pity of War*.

Barker's *Regeneration* joins a long list of fiction that takes the World War I for its setting and theme. Of that lengthy list, several would be of particular interest to readers who enjoyed *Regeneration*. Sebastian Faulks's *Birdsong*, which appeared the year following *Regeneration*, is more epic in its scope, alternating between the years surrounding the war and the late twentieth-century. Faulks's novel takes the reader to the trenches, unlike *Regeneration*, but Faulks shares Barker's close attention to character. Like Barker, Faulks also relies upon the historical Wilfred Owen in crafting his fictional narrative, as does Susan Hill in her novel, *Strange Meeting*. More restricted in its scope than *Birdsong* but sharing Faulks's emphasis on the trenches, Hill offers yet another look at the effects of war on the men who fought it, with an eye towards character. For an alternative version of war through a woman's eyes, consider Helen Zenna Smith's *Not So Quiet* . . . (1930), which follows the experiences of British women ambulance drivers in France and offers a complement to Remarque's male-centered narrative of war, *All Quiet on the Western Front* (1928; trans. 1929).

Though Barker takes the World War I as the focus for her narrative, *Regeneration* is as much about characters under stress and how they learn about themselves through their relationships with others, all told in a fairly realistic narrative style with hints of that which lies beyond understanding. With these themes and styles in mind, readers might also enjoy the work of two authors with whom Barker has identified herself: Gloria Naylor's *Mama Day* and Toni Morrison's *Song of Solomon*. *Mama Day* tells the story of the community of Willows Springs, an island off the coast of Georgia which cannot be found on any map, and its relationship to the "mainland" of the Unites States. Told in first person and third person narratives, the reader follows the characters of Cocoa, George, and the small but powerful Mama Day as they negotiate their relationships to each other and the past. Morrison's *Song of Solomon* follows the literal and figurative journey of Milkman, a young black man, as he discovers his relationship to a past obscured from view and the legacy of his family. Katharine Whittemore in her entry for Pat Barker in *The Salon.com Reader's Guide to Contemporary Authors* (2000) directs readers towards Kazuo Ishiguro and A. S. Byatt, who share Barker's "chameleon-like versatility in style and subject matter" (32). Ishiguro's *The Remains of the Day* and A. S. Byatt's *Angels and Insects: Two Novellas* would be good ones to select: Ishiguro for his psychologically complex rendering of Stevens, the aging butler of a great English manor house who narrates the novel, Byatt for her balance of realistic detail and psychological realism.

Unlike most well-established contemporary authors, Pat Barker does not have many web sites dedicated to her work. Two that are available include one at *The New York Times* and one established for a college course in the United States. *The New York Times* has assembled a page of links to the paper's reviews of Barker's fiction; links to the first chapters of *Another World* and *Border Crossing* are available here, as is a sound file of Barker reading from *Border Crossing*. The page, titled "Featured Author: Pat Barker With News and Reviews From the Archives of *The New York Times*" is available at <http://www.nytimes.com/books/99/05/16/specials/barker.html>. The second site, titled "Pat Barker—Bibliography," features a bibliography of Barker's books and reviews of her work. Assembled to accompany a college course, the page has a link to a brief biography and to study questions as well. The page is available at <http://www.mtmercy.edu/classes/barkerbib.htm>. Though not a full-fledged web resource, a thirty-minute interview with Barker is available in the archives of the National Public Radio program "Fresh Air" at <http://search.npr.org/freshair>. The interview, conducted by "Fresh Air" host Terry Gross, aired on Tuesday, 13 July 1999. Barker discusses her recent novel, *Another World*.

Though the web does not yield much on Barker herself, the web does provide a wealth of information about the time period of *Regeneration*: the First World War. The site developed by "BBC Online" for "World War One" offers a range of resources: a summary of the war years, links to *Daily Mirror* articles about the war, interviews with veterans, a 3-D virtual tour of a trench, and information about making of the UK feature-length television drama "All the King's Men" (1999). The site is available at <http://www.bbc.co.uk/history/war/wwone/index.shtml>.

The setting of *Regeneration* — Craiglockhart in Edinburgh, Scotland — has had a varied history. The building and grounds are now part of Napier University, but Napier University Learning Information Services provides information about its time as Craiglockhart War Hospital. The page "Craiglockhart Connections" at <http://napier.ac.uk/depts/library/craigcon/homepage.htm> offers links to three areas of the site: "The Lands of Craiglockhart" (a history of the land and its buildings), "The War Poets" (links to materials related to Sassoon and Owen), and "Visiting Craiglockhart" (how to arrange a visit to the campus). The second of these three links, "The War Poets," provides a page of links to the library's resources on the war poets, particularly "The Hydra," the literary journal of Craiglockhart War Hospital, of which Owen was an editor during his few months stay. Clicking on the link for "The Hydra" will take the reader to information about the publication and to links of scanned images and the text of the issues themselves.

From "The War Poets" page, readers can also select a link for the page titled "Links to Other Sites," which provides an excellent set of links to information related the First World War, including the Commonwealth War Graves Association, several university sites on the war poets and their poetry, the text of a paper presented by Rivers to the Royal Society of Medicine in 1917, maps and photos of the trenches, and public record information for World War I. The "Links to Other Sites" page also has a link to an incredibly deep resource on Wilfred Owen and the war titled "WOMDA: The Wilfred Owen Multimedia Digital Archive." At WOMDA, readers can find manuscripts for his war poetry, scanned images of his letters, audio interviews with veterans, and about 250 photographs from the war.

Finally, although there are no fan sites devoted to Barker's work, the "Customer Reviews" section at Amazon.com provides a place for readers to exchange views and reviews of her novel. There is a similar, if less active, "Customer Comments" section at Amazon. co.uk and a "Customer Reviews" section at Barnes&Noble.com as well.

QUESTIONS

1. How does the title of Barker's novel, *Regeneration*, reflect the novel's themes?

2. How are the experiments that Rivers and his friend Henry Head performed before the war related to Rivers's work on war neurosis?

3. Many reviewers see Sassoon as the main character of *Regeneration*; Barker says Rivers is the main character. In your opinion, which of *Regeneration*'s characters deserves the title? Why?

4. In an interview with Donna Perry, Barker offers a revealing comment about Prior's character in *Regeneration*: "Prior makes the book, I think. It would be too bland without Prior" (*Backtalk*, 55). What does Prior's character contribute to the novel? Do you agree that he "makes the book" and that it would be "too bland" without him?

5. How would you describe the relationship between Sarah Lumb and Billy Prior? Are they in love? Will their relationship be able to develop further?

6. Rivers believes that Sassoon's poetry and his "Declaration" spring from a similar source. Take a look at the poems Sassoon shares with Rivers in Chapter 3, so Rivers can read them as his "therapist": "The Rear-Guard" (22 April 1917), "The General" (April 1917), and "To the Warmongers" (1917). What do the poems tell us about Sassoon's view of the war? What connections do you see between these poems and the sentiments of Sassoon's "Declaration"?

7. Below is Sassoon's poem "Glory of Women" (1917). Do any of *Regeneration*'s men share the view Sassoon's speaker presents? Do any of *Regeneration*'s women act like the women of the poem?

> You love us when we're heroes, home on leave,
> Or wounded in a mentionable place.
> You worship decorations; you believe
> That chivalry redeems the war's disgrace.
> You make us shells. You listen with delight,
> By tales of dirt and danger fondly thrilled.
> You crown our distant ardours while we fight,
> And mourn our laurelled memories when we're killed.
> You can't believe that British troops "retire"
> When hell's last horror breaks them, and they run,
> Trampling the terrible corpses—blind with blood.
>   O German mother dreaming by the fire,
> While you are knitting socks to send your son
> His face is trodden deeper in the mud.

8. Very few reviewers mention Sarah or the other female characters in their discussions of *Regeneration*—for many, it is as though the female characters aren't even there. What if they weren't there? What is lost by their absence in the novel? What is gained by their inclusion?

9. Why does Rivers fall ill in Chapter 13? What allows him to return to Craiglockhart?

10. At the beginning of Part 3, Rivers sits in church, listening to "Hymn No. 373" which begins: "God moves in a mysterious way." More of the hymn's lyrics appear on the next page. Rivers reflects that this hymn has been popular since the Somme: Why? Does Barker suggest that we are supposed to agree with congregation's response to the hymn?

11. By the end of the novel, does Rivers believe he has done his duty? To whom does he owe this duty?

12. Barker doesn't rely on a lot of description to communicate her ideas, but she does use simile (direct comparisons) and metaphor (indirect comparisons) to great effect. How do such moments of sensory description influence our experience of the characters and the novel? (Consider, for example, when Sassoon is walking at night in Chapter 5 and "the stars burst on his upturned face like spray" or the description of the backstair case Rivers uses at Craiglockhart with pipes "gurgling from time to time like lengths of human intestine.")

13. If possible, watch the film adaptation of Barker's novel. Do you agree with its interpretation of the novel? Does the viewer of the film come away with the same perception of Barker's themes as the reader of the novel?

14. In her interview with Wera Reusch, Barker says that "the historical novel can be a backdoor into the present." How does *Regeneration* provide us with a backdoor into our present culture?

WORKS BY PAT BARKER

Another World. 1998. London: Penguin, 1999.
Blow Your House Down. London: Virago, 1984.
Border Crossing. London: Viking, 2001.
The Eye in the Door. 1993. NY: Penguin, 1995.
The Ghost Road. 1995. NY: Penguin, 1996.
Liza's England. 1986. London: Virago, 1996.
The Man Who Wasn't There. 1989. London: Penguin, 1990.
Regeneration. 1991. NY: Penguin, 1992.
Union Street. London: Virago, 1982.

Notes

1. Sharon Carson's "Pat Barker" and Barker's two interviews with Donna Perry provide the biographical information for this section, unless otherwise indicated.

2. These childhood experiences would find their way into Barker's fiction, particularly *Liza's England* and *The Man Who Wasn't There*.

3. See Ann Ardis's essay, "Political Attentiveness vs. Political Correctness: Teaching Pat Barker's *Blow Your House Down*" (1991), for suggestions on teaching Barker's second novel.

4. Sharon Monteith also notes similarities between Colin and Billy Prior in her essay "Warring Fictions: Reading Pat Barker" and offers a full reading of Barker's early fiction in connection to *Regeneration*.

5. For a fascinating historical analysis of the Booker Prize, see Richard Todd's *Consuming Fictions: The Booker Prize and Fiction in Britain Today* (1996). Todd reads Barker's win as representative of the "heterogeneity of fictional voices in Britain," a diverse atmosphere which the Booker Prize helped to create during the 1980s through its selected winners and short-lists (308–9).

6. Barker identifies Rivers as the main character of the narrative in several interviews, including interviews with Samuel Hynes and Max Davidson.

7. Rivers would consider himself an anthropologist—that is, someone who studies the practices of other cultures—but his methods more closely align him with the newer discipline of ethnography. Ethnography is similar to anthropology, but it is more interested in "thinking and writing about culture from a standpoint of participant observation," as James Clifford states in *The Predicament of Culture* (1988). Unlike anthropological study, which would "aspire to survey the full range of human diversity or development," ethnographic study is "constantly moving *between* cultures," "perpetually displaced" (9).

8. The term "carnivalesque" comes from the work of Mikhail Bakhtin, who theorizes the social dynamic of "carnival" as a time reversals between those who have power and those who lack it, between what is sanctioned and what is taboo. The very fact that the reversals of "carnival" happens as a *prescribed time*, however, indicates that such reversals of power are designed to help a society blow off steam rather than initiate social change.

9. Barker comments on Yelland's methods in an interview with Max Davidson of the *Sunday Telegraph*: "Doctors who used that sort of technique were only doing their best in the light of the medical knowledge of the time." While speaking with Donna Perry, Barker elaborates on the relationship between Rivers and Yelland: "Neither Yelland nor Rivers was really typical, but the balance, at least for the [enlisted] men, was tilted more towards Yelland than Rivers" (*Backtalk* 53).

10. Asked by interviewer Wera Reusch about the difficulty of describing sexuality from a male perspective, Baker responds, with a laugh, "I found Prior a delight to write about and his sexuality is part of this. There was certainly in England at that time a sense among the upper classes that sex was something you did with the lower classes because it belongs to the animal side of your own nature. And Prior is very aware of this and plays on it and plays up to it. But at the same time he very deeply despises it, [. . . .]."

11. Sarah Stickney Ellis, *The Women of England: Their Social Duties and Domestic Habits* (1839), reprinted in *The Norton Anthology of English Literature*, Vol. 2, 7th Edition, eds. M. H. Abrams et al., NY: Norton, 2000, p. 1722. Ellis's book was so popular that it went through sixteen editions in just two years.

12. Joseph Conrad, *Heart of Darkness* (1899), reprinted in *The Norton Anthology of English Literature*, Vol. 2, 7th Edition, eds. M. H. Abrams et al., NY: Norton, 2000, p. 1993. Marlow continues, "We must help them to stay in that beautiful world of their own, lest ours gets worse."

13. After a pause, Barker offers an interesting reading of the relationship between Rivers and Sassoon in an interview with Donna Perry:

> I think, you see, that Rivers is homosexual, too. I think that he is in love with Sassoon. One of the things that can't be said, in fact, is the depth of the feeling he obviously has for Sassoon. Whether he even says it to himself I don't know. There is one time when Sassoon is talking about Owen's feelings for him and these amazing letters that Owen wrote to him. Sassoon thinks that Owen was in love with him and he hopes that he was kind enough, and Rivers simply says, "It happens." That is Rivers with everything hanging out. (*Backtalk* 56)

14. Linda Hutcheon coins the helpful term "historiographic meta-fiction" to identify works that interrogate the boundary between historical reality and fiction. See her study, *The Politics of Postmodernism* (1989), for a much more detailed discussion of the relationship between history and fiction in contemporary writing. Martin Loschnigg's essay addresses these questions in the context of Barker's *Regeneration* trilogy, though he leaves them unresolved by the end of his discussion.

15. I am indebted to my colleague James Campbell for sharing the manuscript of his book, *Strange Meaning: Ethics, Significance, and the First World War*, and its discussion of the close connections between Owen's life narrative and the narrative of *Regeneration*.

16. Notable exceptions are Frances Stead Sellers for *The Washington Post* (3 April 1992) and Melaine Lawrence for *The San Francisco Chronicle* (12 April 1992). Lawrence's review is one of the few (even only one of the daily newspapers) to mention Sarah's character by name.

17. See Todd's *Consuming Fictions*, especially Appendix B, for information about how a Booker win typically affects sales.

18. The "Diary" for the *Sunday Times* (26 May 1991) briefly mentions that George Sassoon accused Barker "of basing her depiction of his famous father too closely in Sassoon's autobiographical novel, *The Complete Memoirs of George Sherston*." Barker's publishers and agents quickly dismissed

such charges of copyright violation and, it seems, won, since no more was heard of George Sassoon's challenge.

19. Although Amazon.co.uk has a section for "Customer Comments," it only went into place in 1999. Most readers, whether from the US or the UK or other countries, tend to post to the original site at Amazon.com. As of March 2001, there were 28 reviews posted, some quite lengthy, the first review was posted in August 1996 and the most recent review was posted in November 2000.

Works Cited

Abrams, M. H. et al. *The Norton Anthology of British Literature*. Vol. 2.,
7th ed. NY: Norton, 2000.

Andrews, Nigel. "Rhetoric Rather Than Reality." *Financial Times*, 20 Nov
1997: 17.

Ardis, Ann. "Political Attentiveness vs. Political Correctness: Teaching Pat
Barker's *Blow Your House Down.*" *College Literature*, 18. 3 Oct 1991:
44–54.

Becker, Alida. "Old War Wounds: An Interview." *New York Times
Book Review*, 16 May 1999: 23 Jan 2001. <http://www.nytimes.com/
books>

de Bertodano, Helena. "Booker Prize Blows Her Cover." *Sunday Telegraph*,
12 Nov 1995: 3.

Billson, Anne. "Some Things Movies Can't Handle." *Sunday Telegraph*,
23 Nov 1997: 11.

Carson, Sharon. "Pat Barker." *British Writers*. Supplement IV. Eds. George
Stade and Carol Howard. NY: Scribner's, 1997: 45–63.

Clifford, James. *The Predicament of Culture*. Cambridge, MA: Harvard
University Press, 1988.

"Customer Comments." *"Regeneration,* Pat Barker." Amazon.co.uk., 27 March 2001. <http://www.amazon,co.uk>

"Customer Reviews." *"Regeneration* by Pat Barker." Amazon.com., 27 March 2001. <http://www.amazon.com>

"Customer Reviews—An Open Forum." *"Regeneration,* Pat Barker." Barnes & Noble.com., 29 March 2001. <http://www.barnesandnoble.com>

Davidson, Max. "The ghosts of war march again." *Sunday Telegraph,* 16 Nov. 1997: 11.

Davis, Clive. "Anthems for Doomed Youth." *The Times,* 28 Nov 1991.

"Diary." *The Sunday Times,* 26 May 1991.

Dickson, E. Jane. "Transfixed by the Bloody Battlefield." *The Times,* 11 Nov 2000.

"Dougray Scott in *Regeneration.*" Dougray.net. 29 March 2001. <http://www.dougray.net/regen/regeneration.html>

Feay, Suzi. "Catalogue of Excess." *The Independent,* 7 Jan 2001: 41–43.

Ferguson, Niall. "Do Today's Public Rituals Hinder Our Understanding of War?" *The Independent,* 11 Nov 1998: 4.

French, Philip. "Film of the Week." *The Observer,* 30 Nov 1997: 69.

Goring, Rosemary. "At War with Words." *Scotland on Sunday,* 25 Oct 1998: 29.

Gritten, David. "Battle for Men's Minds." *The Daily Telegraph,* 21 Nov 1997: 24.

Grove, Valerie. "I Know in My Bones that Book Prizes Are Just Three Lemons in a Row."*The Times,* 29 Sept 1995.

Harris, Michael. "In Brief: Fiction." *Los Angeles Times,* 12 April 1992: 6.

Hartl, John. " 'Regeneration': Sharing Some of Ryan's Concerns." *The Seattle Times,* 21 Aug 1998: G4.

Hensher, Philip. "Getting Better All the Time." *The Guardian,* 26 Nov 1993: S4.

Herman, David. "No Peace for War's 'Goddamned Cowards.' " *The Independent,* 5 Dec 2000: 5.

Hoffman, Eva. "The Super Bowl of Fiction." *New York Times Book Review,* 26 Nov 1995; 23 Jan 2001. <http://www.nytimes.com/books>

Hynes, Samuel. "Among Damaged Men." *New York Times Book Review,* 29 March 1992: 1.

"Introduction." Contemporary English Literature Web Site. Highland Council Education Service. 16 Jan 2001 <http://members.tripod.co.uk/highlandschools/intro.htm>

Johnston, Trevor. "Haunted by the Frontline." *The Scotsman*, 1 Jan 1998: 10.

Kemp, Peter. "Getting Under the Skin of a Nation at War." *Sunday Times*, 2 June 1991.

Lawrence, Melanie. "Poetry, Conscience." *San Franscisco Chronicle*, 12 April 1992: 8.

Loschnigg, Martin. " ' . . . the novelist's responsibility to the past': History, Myth, and the Narratives of Crisis in Pat Barker's *Regeneration* Trilogy (1991–1995)." *Zeitschrift fur Anglistik und Amerikanistik* 47.3, 1999: 214–228.

Maslin, Janet. "A Doctor and a Poet Transformed by a War." *New York Times*, 14 August 1998: E10.

McCartney, Jennifer. "Women Only?" *Sunday Telegraph*, 23 April 2000: 21.

McCrum, Robert, "It's a Disaster for a Novel to Be Topical." *The Observer*, 1 April 2001.

Mitgang, Herbert. "Healing a Mind and Spirit Badly Wounded in the Trenches."*New York Times*, 15 April 1992: C21.

Monteith, Sharon. "Warring Fictions: Reading Pat Barker." *Moderna spreak*, 91.2 (1997): 124–139.

O'Connell, Dee. "Life Support." *The Observer*, 4 March 2001: 70.

"Pat Barker's Answers to Readers' Questions." *The Guardian*. 28 April 2001. <http://booktalk.guardian.co.uk>

Perry, Donna. "Going Home Again: An Interview with Pat Barker." *The Literary Review: An International Journal of Contemporary Writing*. 34:2 (Winter 1991): 235–44. Gale Literature Resource Center. 18 February 2001. <http://www.galenet.com>

———. "Pat Barker." *Backtalk: Women Writers Speak Out*. New Brunswick, NJ: Rutgers UP, 1993. 43–61.

Picardie, Justine. "The Poet Who Came Out of His Shell Shock." *The Independent*, 25 June 1991: 19.

Pierpoint, Claudia Roth. "Shell Shock." *The New York Times Book Review*, 31 Dec 1995. 23 Jan 2001. <http://www.nytimes.com/books>

Quinn, Anthony. "What Sassoon Could Never Resolve." *Daily Telegraph*, 2 Sept 1995: 4.

Ray, Kevin. "Poets in a Time of Death." *St. Louis Post-Dispatch*, 26 April 1992: 5C.

"Regeneration." Internet Movie Database. 29 March 2001. <http://www.imdb.com>

"Regeneration Game." *The Guardian*. 21 Nov 1997: 9.

Reusch, Wera. "A Backdoor into the Present: An Interview with Pat Barker." 2000. Trans. Heather Batchelor. *LOLA Press*. 16 Jan 2001 <http://www.lolapress.org/reue.htm>

Rodd, Candice. "A Stomach for War." *The Independent*, 12 Sept 1993: 28.

Sachs, Lloyd. "Poetic Injustice."*The Chicago Sun-Times*, 21 Aug 1998: 35.

Sammon, Geof. "Pat Barker, a Modern British Writer."*Neusprachliche Mitteinlungen aus Wissenschaft und Praxis*, 49: 1 (1996): 42–44.

Sellers, Frances Stead. "The Poet of the Trenches." *The Washington Post*, 3 April 1992: D1.

Shephard, Ben. "Digging Up the Past." *Times Literary Supplement* 4851, 1996: 12–13.

Shilling, Jane. "Shaking Off the Ghosts of War." *The Daily Telegraph*, 24 Oct 1998: 5.

Smith, Amanda. Interview with Pat Barker. *Publishers Weekly*, 21 Sept 1984: 98–9. The Gale Literature Resource Center. 18 February 2001. <http://www.galenet.com>

Stoffman, Judy. "Still Clearing Away the World Wars Debris." *The Toronto Star*. 30 Dec 1998.

Talyor, Paul. "Hero at the Emotional Front." *The Independent*, 2 June 1991: 32.

Thomas, Kevin. "Cerebral Look at War's Toll." *Los Angeles Times*, 14 Aug 1998: F8.

Thorpe, Vanessa. "Literary Love Is for Girls and Sissies." *The Observer*, 19 March 2000. Guardian Unlimited. 29 March 2001. <http://books.guardian.co.uk>

Todd, Richard. *Consuming Fictions: The Booker Prize and Fiction in Britain Today*. London: Bloomsbury, 1996.

Upchurch, Michael. "Books Briefly." *The Seattle Times*, 21 June 1992: K6.

Whittemore, Katharine. "Barker, Pat." *The Salon.com Reader's Guide to Contemporary Authors*. Eds. Laura Miller and Adam Begley. NY: Penguin, 2000. 31–2.

Wilson, Jean Moorcroft. "Lines from the Front." *The Times*, 10 Nov 2000.

Wullschlager, Jackie. "Sanity, Madness and Unholy Innocence." *Financial Times*, 6 July 1991: ix.

Wyatt-Brown, Anne M. "Headhunters and Victims of the War: W. H. R. Rivers and Pat Barker." *Proceedings from the Thirteenth International Conference on Literature and Psychoanalysis*. Ed. Frederico Pereira. 1996. Lisbon: Instituto Superior de Psicologia Aplicada, 1997. 53–59.